# A Splash of Fall

by
**Susanne Glover**
**and**
**Georgeann Grewe**

**illustrated by Georgeann Grewe**

Cover by Vanessa Filkins

Copyright © Good Apple, Inc., 1987

ISBN No. 0-86653-410-5

Printing No. 987654321

**GOOD APPLE, INC.**
**BOX 299**
**CARTHAGE, ILLINOIS 62321-0299**

Cover by Vanessa Filkins

Copyright © Good Apple, Inc., 1987

ISBN No. 0-86653-410-5

Printing No. 987654321

**GOOD APPLE, INC.**
**BOX 299**
**CARTHAGE, ILLINOIS 62321-0299**

# Table of Contents

# COME "FALL"OW

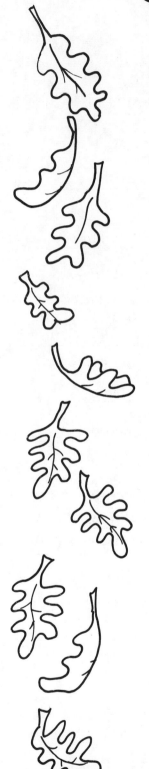

SPLASH ME RED! SPLASH ME GREEN!
SPLASH ME YELLOW—WHAT A BEAUTIFUL SCENE!
AS AUTUMN COLORS BEGIN TO UNFOLD,
AS SUMMER WINDS TURN CHILLY AND COLD,
YOUR ROOM WILL BE PAINTED WITH BRIGHTFULNESS OF
    FALL
WITH THESE UNITS GALORE FOR BOTH BIG KIDS AND
    SMALL.
COME! COLOR YOUR DAY! CAPTURE A CHILD'S HEART.
TRY THESE FUN-FULLED IDEAS: GET A BRAND-NEW START!

# TEACHER TIPS

**WELCOME, CLASS** (page 1)
* Make this wreath decoration by using the patterns included for October and November. Add patterns of your own for variety.

**APPLECADABRA** (pages 10-12)
* Duplicate this game for each child or simply use it as a station to supplement your teaching of this skill.
* Use this game as part of the BAG IT unit. Make copies of this gameboard and pieces for all students so they may put them in Ziploc bags and store it in their BAG.

**STATIONERY** (page 14)
* Give children this form to write home about their progress.
* Assign work to be completed on this paper to use as a display on a bulletin board or for something special.

**BAG IT** (pages 15-18)
* Extend the bulletin board theme to include an all-day unit for the first day or two of school. Give each student a large brown grocery bag to decorate. Then incorporate all of the content areas included in this section. Provide each student with several Ziploc bags for storing his work in his bag. A few of these activities can be used throughout the entire year. Choose lessons suitable for your grade level or adapt them to suit your needs.

**COPYCAT** (page 42)
* Read and discuss the poem orally with the class, discussing format, rhyme, capital letters and punctuation before assigning children to copy the poem in their best writing.

**STOP 'N GO STRIPS** (pages 43-44)
* Make several copies of the stoplight pattern. Laminate it after you color it. Duplicate several strips in various colors, with each color representing a particular content area or a particular level of difficulty. Stoplights can then be stored in color-coded envelopes for easy identification when various skills are studied.

**AUTUMN "TREE"T** (pages 45-48)
* Prepare an all-day unit of study by combining various activities found in this section which are appropriate to your level.
* Establish the mood in your classroom for your unit by building a small library using topics from Branching Out or others you find in your school library.

**DELIGHTFUL "BITEFULL"** (pages 65-69)
* Use this bulletin board for a variety of concepts! It can easily be adapted to any type of skill where matching is involved. Introduce your students to this candy apple theme by making this treat with or for your students.

**A GREAT CLASS, STARRING . . .** (pages 79-80)
* Display a picture of each student and use the Door Knocker as a bulletin board welcoming students to your classroom.
* Change the hat on the moon to represent another season so that the display can be used in various ways.
* Arrange the stars to make different constellations on a wall inside your classroom.

**TEEPEE TRIVIA** (pages 96-98)
* Challenge your students with this Indian unit. Choose appropriate activities so that all students can be motivated. A complete study of Indians is included so that research is guided with a variety of activities. Use the Indian program found in this section as a culminating activity for your own class and a learning experience for others who are invited.
* Make a large teepee in your classroom to create interest in this Indian study.
* Allow for individual research by reviewing library skills: taking notes, finding sources for reports, writing a report, writing a bibliography, making an outline.
* Encourage group work by assigning group leaders and allowing leaders to guide group members through productive yet fun activities. Use the contract and certificate provided to "make it official."
* Inspire your students to explore the arts as they make drums, musical instruments, costumes, etc. Provide time to learn play parts and make props for a successful performance.
* Invite community members, neighbors, parents to the celebration.
* Display completed projects throughout the school for other students to see or plan an exhibit for parent-teacher conferences.


Slight preparations may be necessary as the activities are adapted to the needs of your classroom. You may wish to supplement with some of your own ideas and materials.

**TO CREATE THE BULLETIN BOARD, YOU WILL NEED:**

1.  A large sheet of yellow background paper.
2.  Patterns for the letters in the title, which can be found on the following two pages.
3.  Red and/or green construction paper for the apple patterns which follow.
4.  A large red bow for the wreath, either real for 3-D effect or a flat paper bow.

**PRACTICAL USES:**

1.  Write the name of each student in your class on an apple. Use the bulletin board as a display to welcome students into your classroom.
2.  Attach a school picture to the child's apple with his name on it.
3.  Give each student a construction paper apple. Read the story of Johnny Appleseed to your class. On the back of his apple, have each student write a summary of that story.
4.  Give each child a paper apple. Have him write a recipe for an apple "goodie" on it. Display recipes for all to see. Ask students to bring in samples of their recipes for others to taste.
*5. Use the October or November patterns in this section to create a classroom wreath for the fall season. Change the bulletin board title to "Welcome, October!" or "Welcome, November!"

2

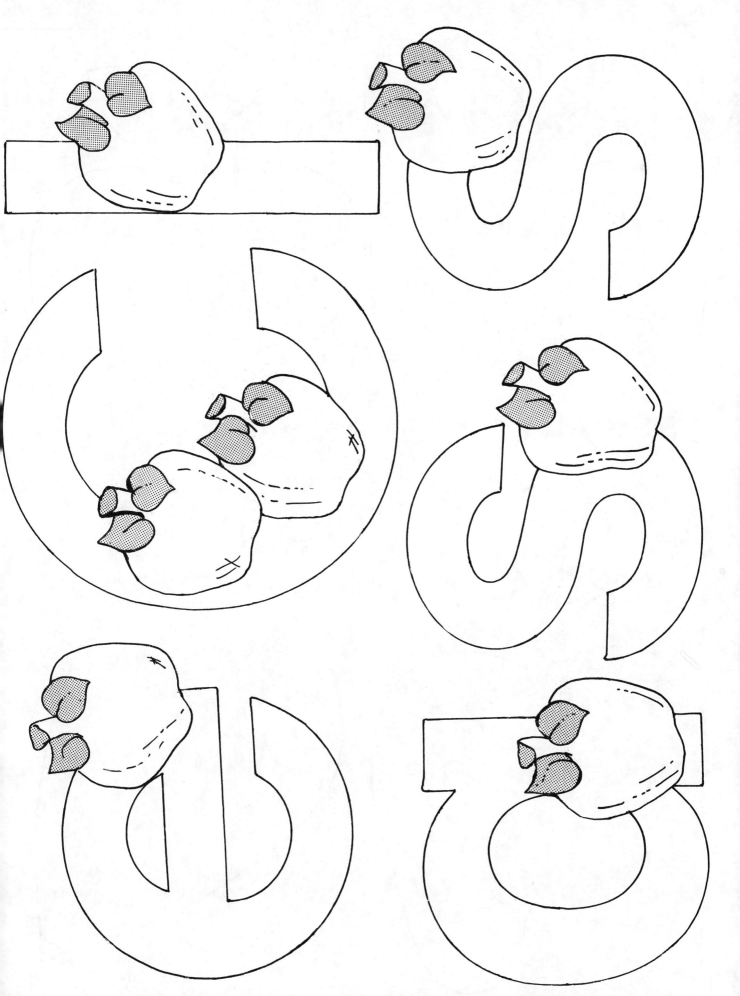

6

# MY CLASS SCHEDULE

**NAME:**                              **TEACHER:**

| Time | Monday | Tuesday | Wednesday | Thursday | Friday |
|------|--------|---------|-----------|----------|--------|
|      |        |         |           |          |        |
|      |        |         |           |          |        |
|      |        |         |           |          |        |
|      |        |         |           |          |        |
|      |        |         |           |          |        |
|      |        |         |           |          |        |
|      |        |         |           |          |        |
|      |        |         |           |          |        |
|      |        |         |           |          |        |
|      |        |         |           |          |        |

# Incredible Edibles

1. 504
   -328

2. 931
   -649

3. 862
   -573

4. 407
   -219

5. 631
   -495

6. 725
   -186

7. 801
   -477

8. 930
   -571

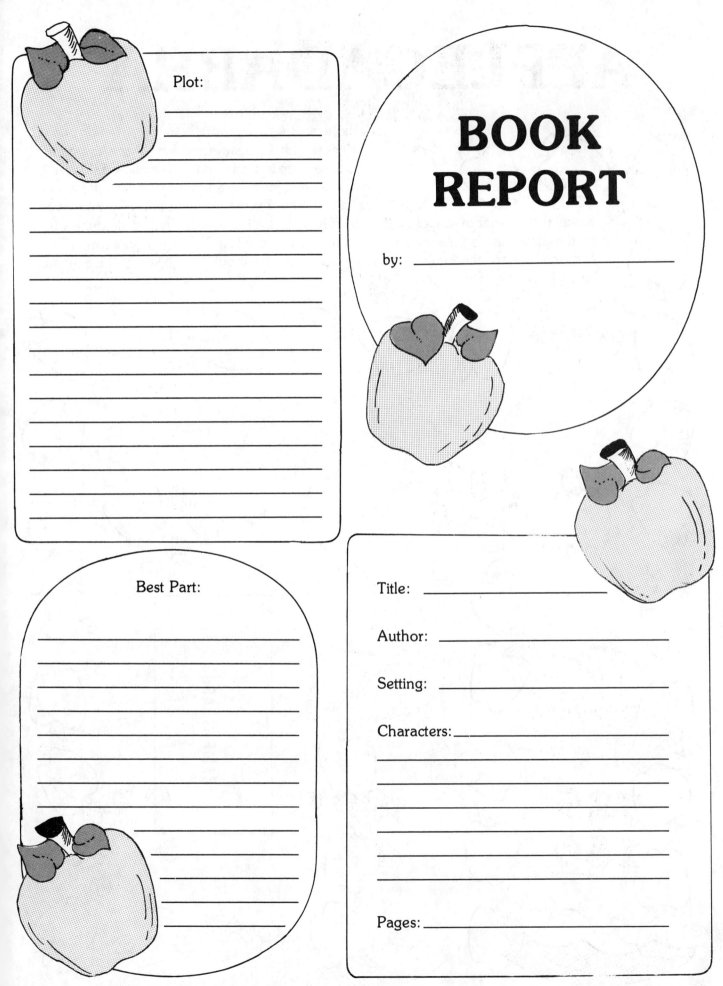

Plot:

_____

BOOK REPORT

by: _____

Best Part:

_____

Title: _____

Author: _____

Setting: _____

Characters: _____

_____

Pages: _____

# APPLECADABRA

START

**Players:** 2-4

**Directions:** Choose a marker. Place the game cards face up in a pile on the gameboard. Player 1 rolls the die. He then takes a game card. If he correctly abbreviates the word on the card, he moves ahead the number of spaces on the die. If he answers incorrectly, he remains where he is. If a player lands on a worm, he must go back to START. Players take turns. The first one to reach the END wins the game. (Answers should be on the backs of game cards.)

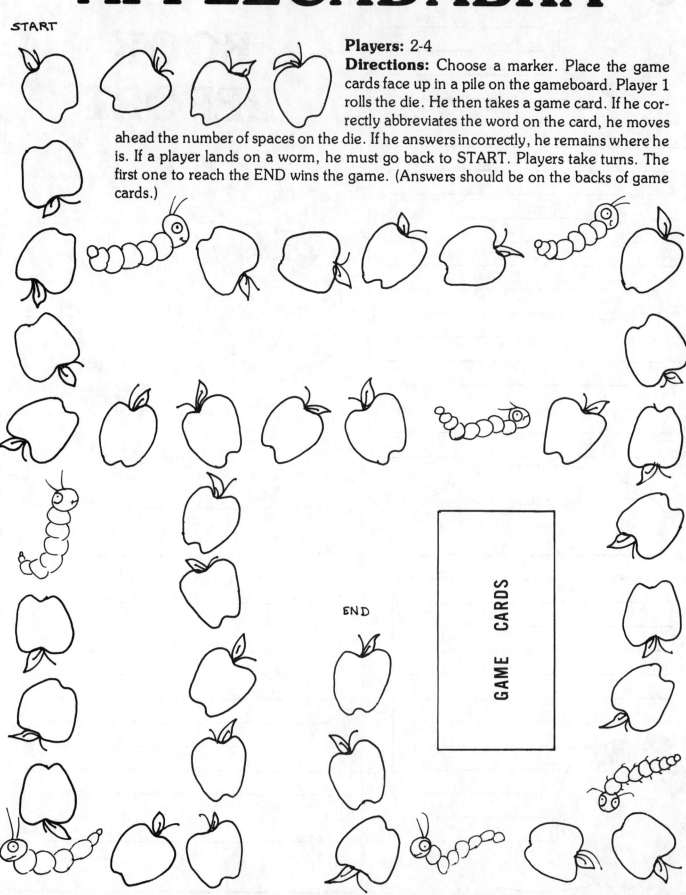

END

GAME CARDS

10

| Sunday | Monday | Tuesday |
|---|---|---|
| Wednesday | Thursday | Friday |
| Saturday | January | February |
| March | April | May |
| June | July | August |
| September | October | November |
| December | Mister | Missus |
| Miss | Reverend | Doctor |

| President | Prime Minister | General |
|---|---|---|
| Captain | Ante Meridian | Post Meridian |
| Street | Road | Avenue |
| Boulevard | Route | Drive |
| inch | foot | yard |
| mile | dozen | pound |
| month | week | year |
| number | Junior | Senior |

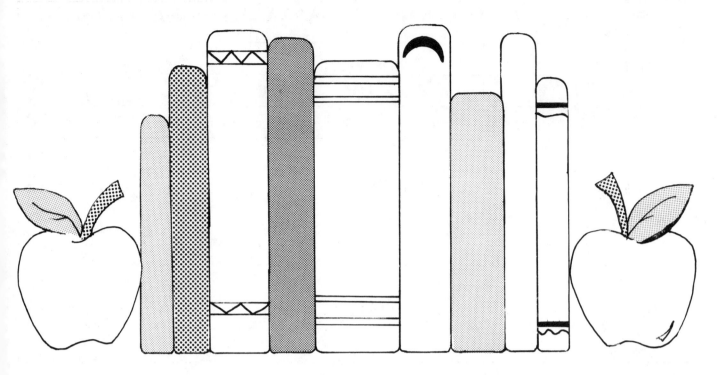

# YOU'RE THE LIBRARIAN!

Follow these simple directions as you arrange the books above in your library. Read each step carefully before you decide what to do!

1. PRINT your first and last name on the tallest book.

2. Count four books over from the left side. COLOR this book red.

3. The thickest book on the shelf is Webster's Dictionary. WRITE its name on it.

4. The second book from the right end is yellow. COLOR it. Then WRITE the numbers 1-10 on it.

5. The shortest book is Spelling. LABEL it.

6. PRINT your initials on each book end. COLOR the apples.

7. The book to the left of the red book is a cookbook. WRITE *Cookbook* on it.

8. Between the Cookbook and the Spelling book is a blue book. COLOR it.

9. To the right of the yellow book is a book about your teacher. PRINT your teacher's name on it.

10. The third book from the right end is an animal book. WRITE your favorite animal on its side, followed by the word MYSTERY.

BAG IT

## TO CREATE THE BULLETIN BOARD, YOU WILL NEED:

1. A large sheet of light-blue background paper.
2. Patterns for the letters in the title which can be found on the following page.
3. A large brown grocery bag for the teacher and enough smaller brown bags for each student in your class.
4. Patterns of the face, arms, and legs for each student, made from construction paper (pages 16-18).
5. Ziploc bags for the activities found within the BAG IT unit.

## PRACTICAL USES:

1. Ask each child to complete his grocery bag as you have decorated yours for the bulletin board. His bag will be smaller and can be used to store all of the activities he completes the first day or two of school. Later it can be attached to the bulletin board with yours.
2. Because of the versatility of this bulletin board, use it for any content area.
3. Use the bulletin board as a station or a center for a manipulative type activity and schedule students into it.

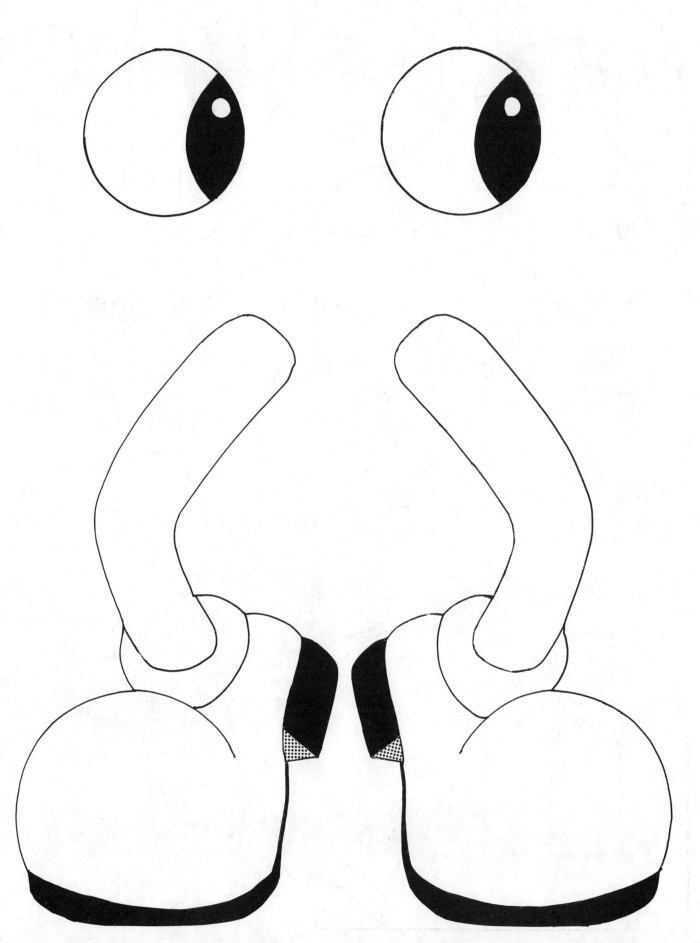

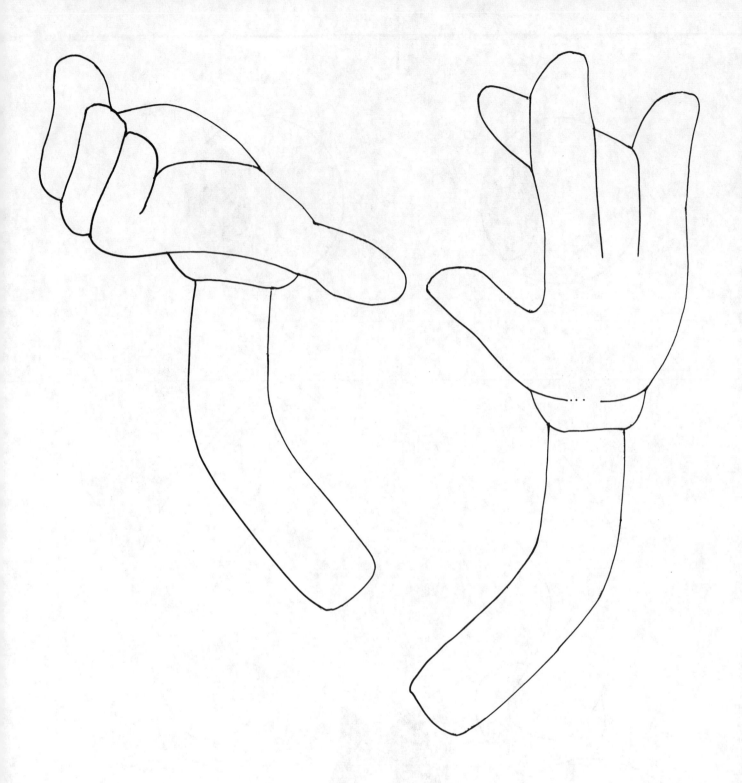

TIME
for
SCHOOL

19

# SACK LUNCH

Give each child patterns for the food and the money (pages 20-22). Have him cut out all patterns and place them on his desk. Give a Ziploc bag to each chld. Ask him to add up his lunch (use all food pieces) and place the correct amount of money in his bag. Then give each child a LUNCH BAG MATH work sheet. Have him tabulate the cost of each lunch and write the correct amount on the bag. (You may wish to use two pages of money patterns per child to add more variety.)

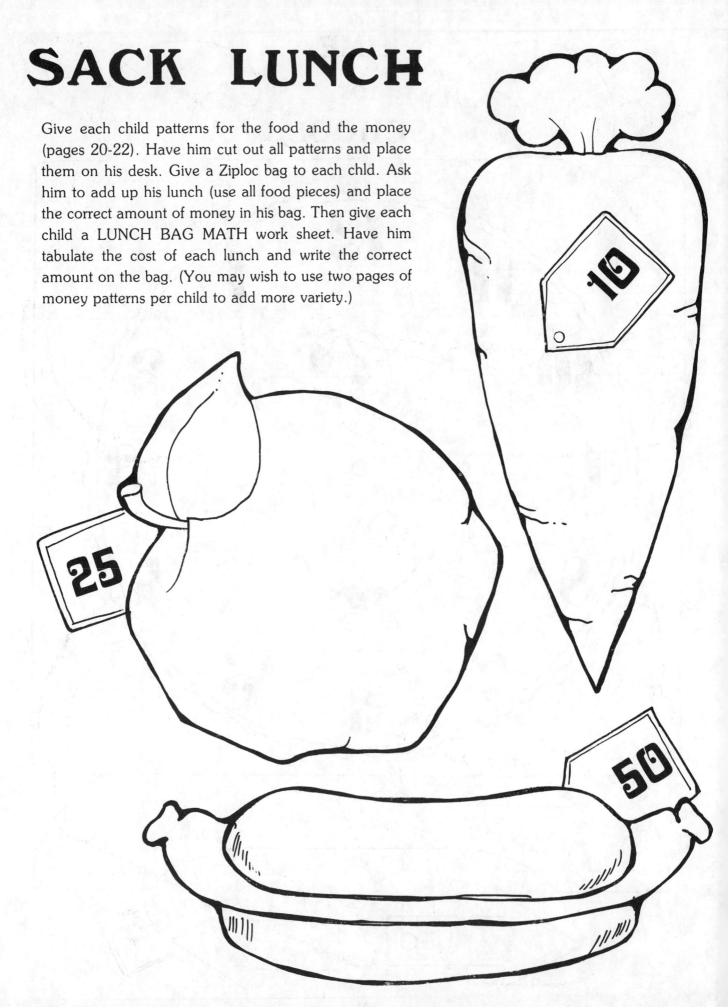

| | | |
|---|---|---|
| 10 | 50 | 5 |
| 25 | 10 | 25 |
| 5 | 25 | 10 |
| 10 | 10 | 25 |
| 25 | 25 | 10 |

# LUNCH BAG MATH

**WALT**

    2   HAMBURGERS
    1   CARROT
    1   PEAR
    1   ICE-CREAM CONE
    _____

Total :

**ANN**

    1   HOT DOG
    3   CARROTS
        PIE
    _____

Total :

**JUDY**

    1   HAMBURGER
    1   HOT DOG
    1   APPLE
    1   ICE-CREAM CONE
    _____

Total :

# A Nature Scavenger Hunt

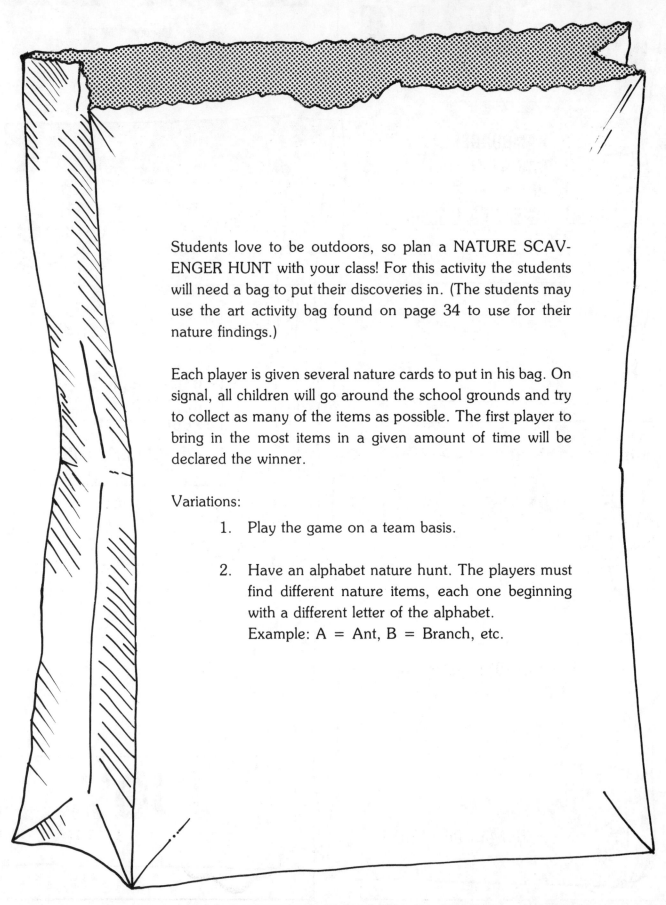

Students love to be outdoors, so plan a NATURE SCAVENGER HUNT with your class! For this activity the students will need a bag to put their discoveries in. (The students may use the art activity bag found on page 34 to use for their nature findings.)

Each player is given several nature cards to put in his bag. On signal, all children will go around the school grounds and try to collect as many of the items as possible. The first player to bring in the most items in a given amount of time will be declared the winner.

Variations:

1.  Play the game on a team basis.

2.  Have an alphabet nature hunt. The players must find different nature items, each one beginning with a different letter of the alphabet.
    Example: A = Ant, B = Branch, etc.

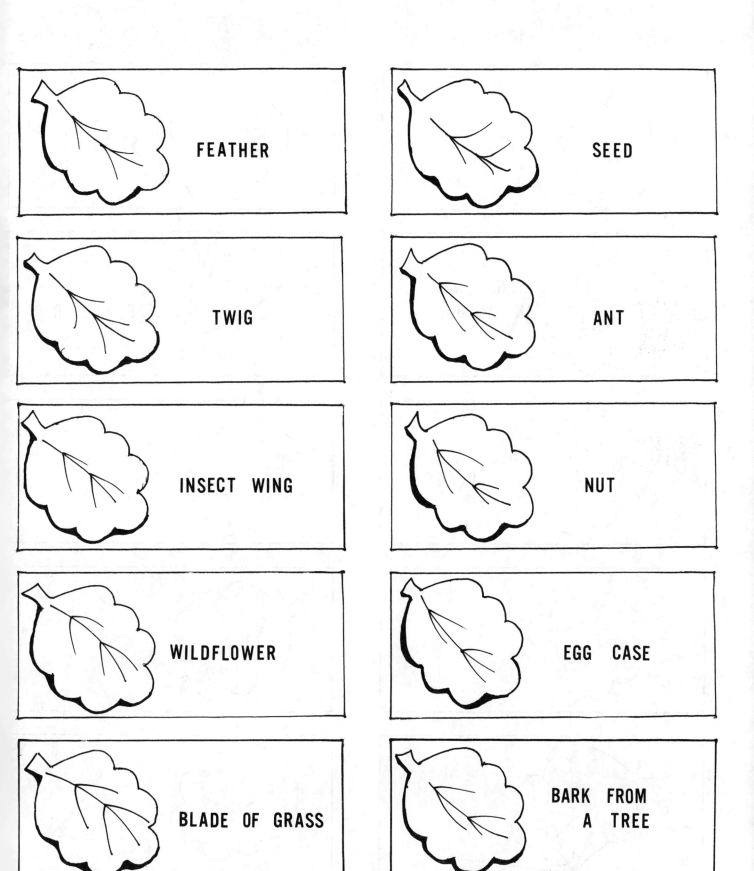

FEATHER

SEED

TWIG

ANT

INSECT WING

NUT

WILDFLOWER

EGG CASE

BLADE OF GRASS

BARK FROM
A TREE

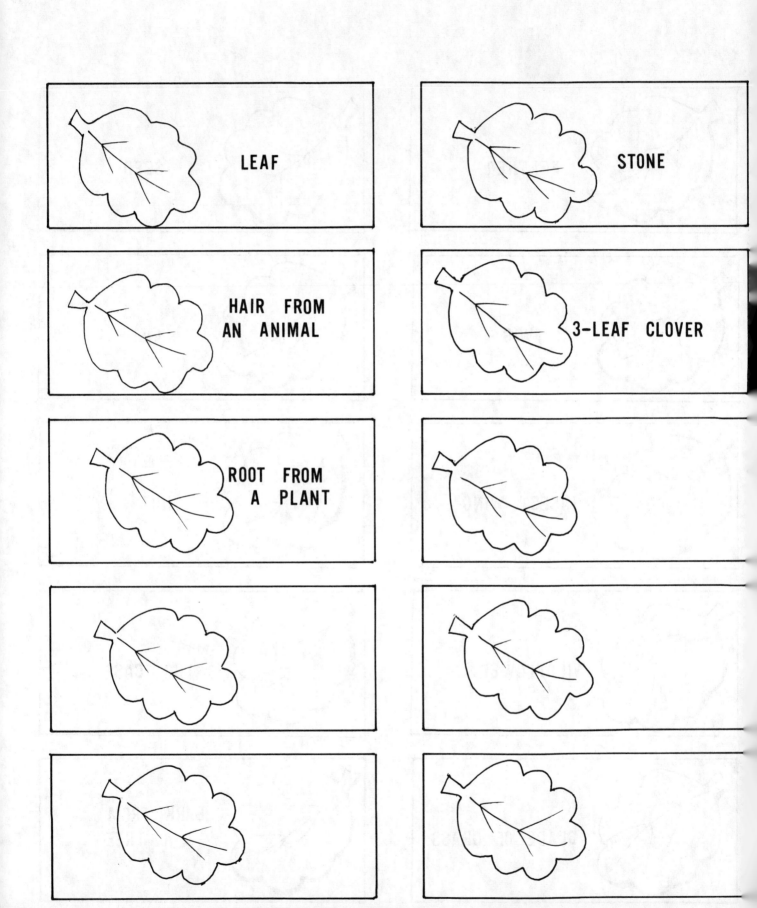

LEAF

STONE

HAIR FROM
AN ANIMAL

3-LEAF CLOVER

ROOT FROM
A PLANT

I GO TO

_____ SCHOOL.

MY PRINCIPAL IS _____.

MY TEACHERS ARE:

_____

_____

_____

_____

_____

I AM IN THE _____ GRADE.

# MARVELOUS ME

27

WHEN I WAS LITTLE I _____

_____

_____

MY FAVORITE PLACE IS _____

_____

WHEN I GROW UP I WANT TO BE A _____

BECAUSE _____

_____

This is ME now. Age _____

---

MY NAME IS _____

I WAS BORN IN _____
city

I LIVE IN A _____ WITH MY _____

MY EYES ARE _____ AND MY HAIR
IS _____

MY FAVORITE FOOD IS _____

MY FAVORITE HOBBIES ARE _____

_____

_____

I COLLECT _____

MY FAVORITE SUBJECT IS _____

28

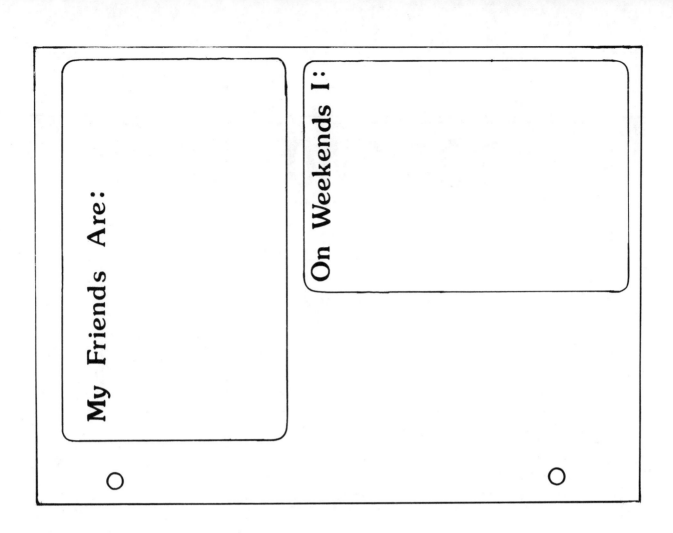

My Friends Are:

On Weekends I:

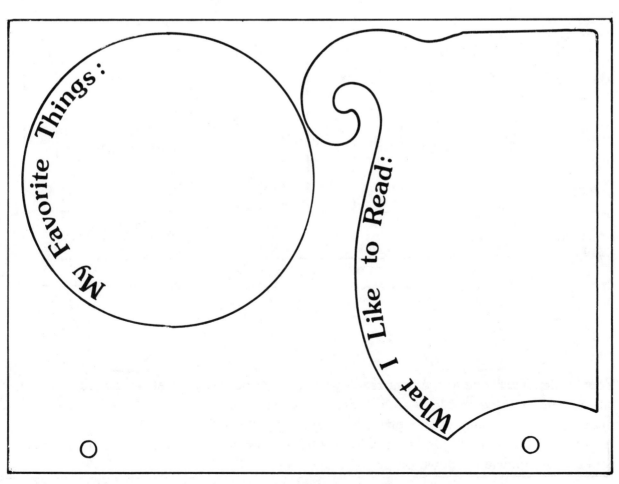

My Favorite Things:

What I Like to Read:

# BOOKMOBILE

NAME: _____

Your students will love to see their reading progress using this decorative hanging. Give an oaktag pattern of the mobile to each student. Have him write his name on the bumper. As a student finishes reading a book, give him an oaktag pattern of a book. Ask him to write the title on it and illustrate it. On the back of the book have him write a brief summary. Attach books to the mobile as shown on page 31.

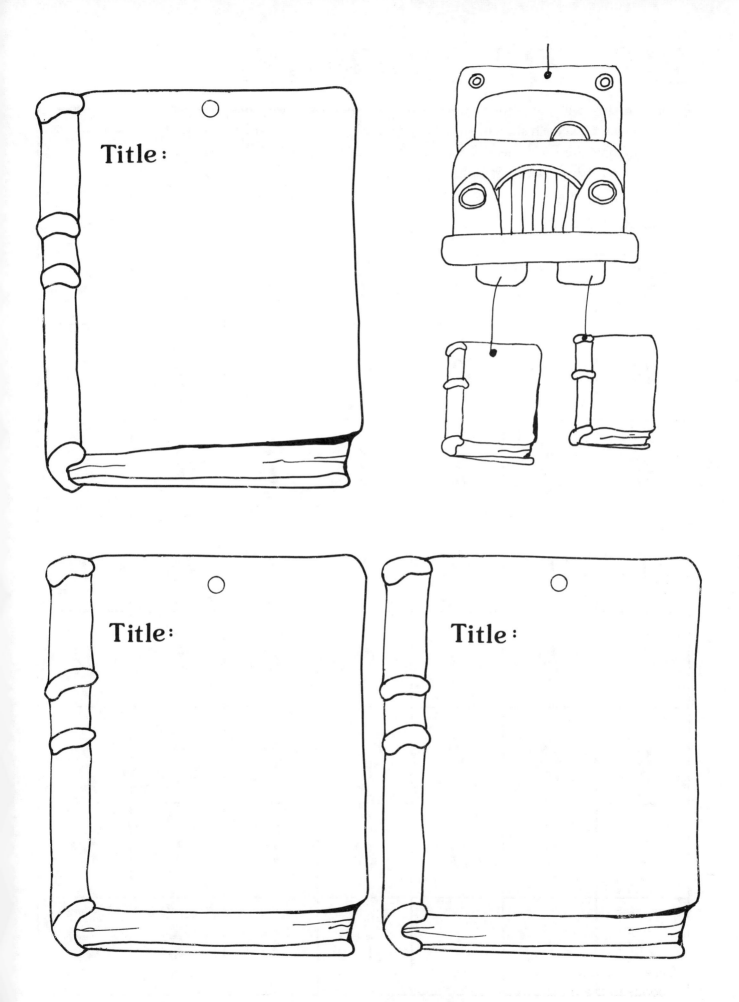

Title:

Title:

Title:

# ZIP ZIP HOORAY!

Your students will have their SPELLING "in the bag" with this compact manipulative. Give each student an oaktag copy of this page. After he cuts apart the letters, have him store his alphabet in a Ziploc bag. Group activities might include: (1) teaching/reviewing alphabetical order for a few or all of the letters; (2) "writing" spelling words in competition; (3) composing brief sentences.

| | | | | | | |
|---|---|---|---|---|---|---|
| | | | | | | *a* |

| | | | | | | |
|---|---|---|---|---|---|---|
| *a* | *a* | *b* | *b* | *c* | *c* | *d* |
| *d* | *e* | *e* | *e* | *f* | *f* | *g* |
| *g* | *h* | *h* | *i* | *i* | *i* | *j* |
| *j* | *k* | *k* | *l* | *l* | *m* | *m* |
| *n* | *n* | *o* | *o* | *o* | *p* | *p* |
| *q* | *q* | *r* | *r* | *s* | *s* | *t* |
| *t* | *u* | *u* | *u* | *v* | *v* | *w* |
| *w* | *x* | *x* | *y* | *y* | *z* | *z* |

# Speeding Through SPELLING

Copy any fourteen of your spelling words for the week into the blocks of the puzzle. Lightly color it before you cut it out. Try to work it a few times before you trade with your friend. Keep your puzzle in an envelope. Study all of your words for your test! This could also be used with the BAG IT unit. Have students store puzzle in Ziploc bag.

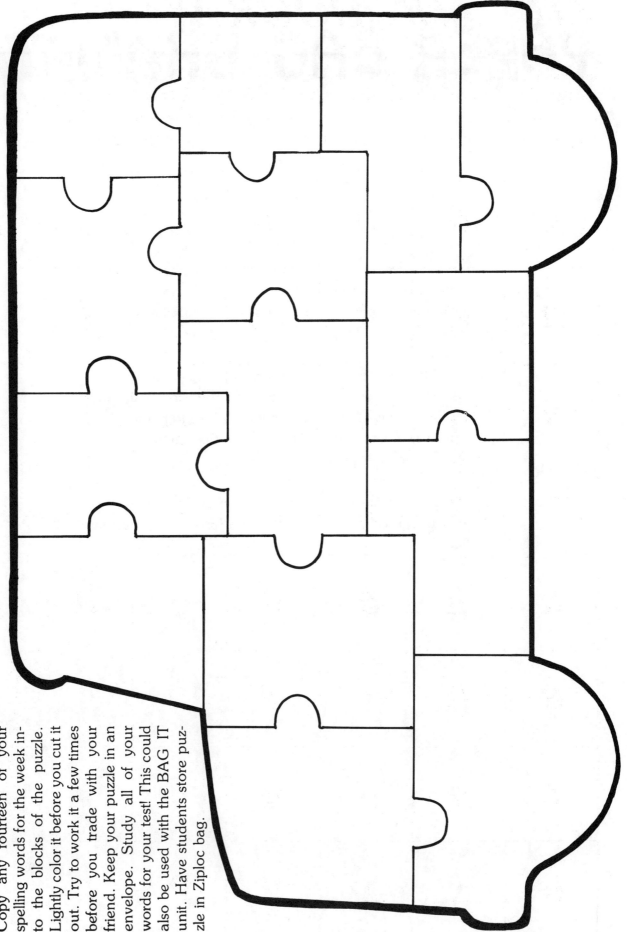

# PAPER BAG DRAMATICS

Get five large brown grocery bags. Fill each one with various old household items. Each bag should contain eight to ten objects, with each bag being different from the others.

Divide your class into groups of approximately five students. Give each team a bag which you have prepared. Allow teams twenty minutes or so to prepare and practice a skit using all of the items in the bag. Invite other groups to your presentations.

As an alternative, allow students to provide various items for the grocery bags. Save this fun for a rainy or winter day!

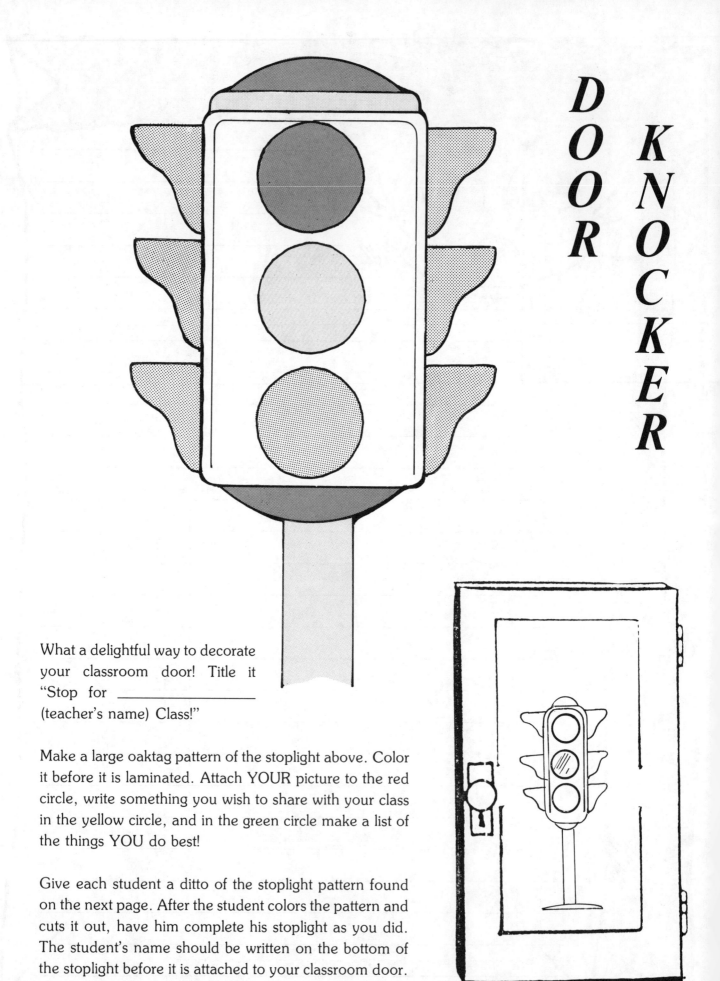

## DOOR KNOCKER

What a delightful way to decorate your classroom door! Title it "Stop for _____ (teacher's name) Class!"

Make a large oaktag pattern of the stoplight above. Color it before it is laminated. Attach YOUR picture to the red circle, write something you wish to share with your class in the yellow circle, and in the green circle make a list of the things YOU do best!

Give each student a ditto of the stoplight pattern found on the next page. After the student colors the pattern and cuts it out, have him complete his stoplight as you did. The student's name should be written on the bottom of the stoplight before it is attached to your classroom door.

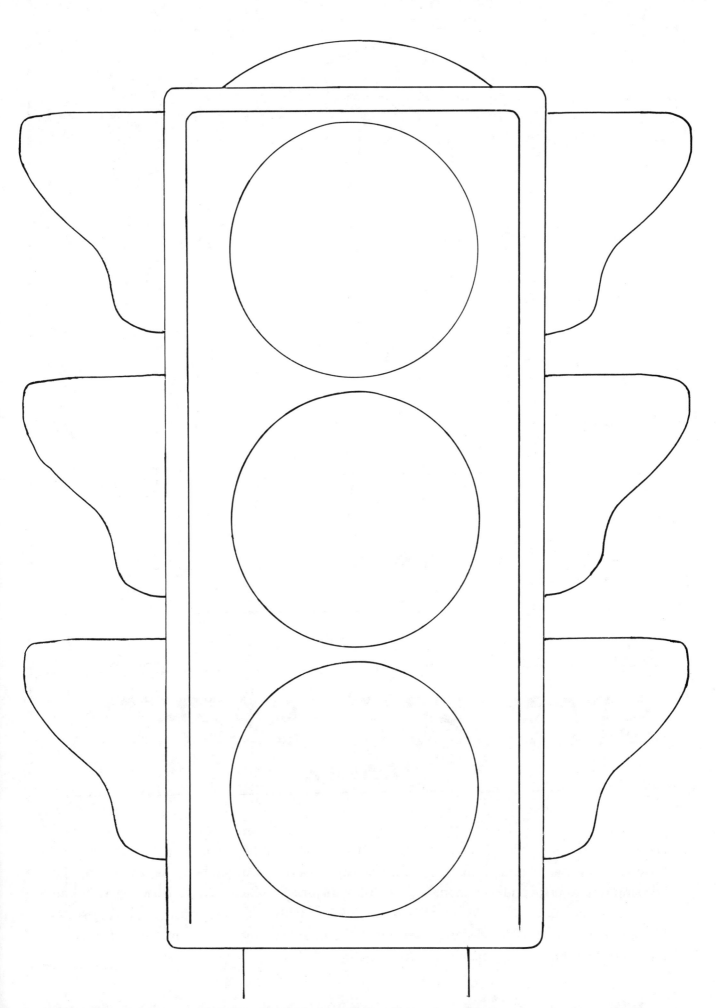

# STOP FOR SAFETY

### HEALTH

Here's a great activity which involves the entire class! Use it later as a small group or partner activity to review health and safety rules. Get a sturdy envelope. Cut out both the picture and the title strip on this page and glue them to the front of the envelope. Cut apart the stop signs found on the following pages and place them inside. Your students will enjoy preparing their answers to their own cards as well as listening to other children explain their situations. Allow for lots of discussion. Add topics of your own if you like!

# STOP!
# for Health and Safety

1. When you are inside a building, why should you talk softly to your friends?

2. If you are a school patrol, what steps would you follow if a student does not listen to you?

3. Why should you tell your teacher or adult in charge if you are allergic to something?

4. What can you do while sitting at your school desk if you notice that your eyes feel tired?

5. Why is it important to flush the toilet and wash your hands after using the bathroom?

6. If you bring medicine to school after you have been ill, what should you do with it? Why?

7. If you have been doing your homework and you begin to feel stress, what are four things that you could do?

8. If you see someone on the playground who is hurt, what should you do? Why?

9. Can you name the various food groups that are usually found on a school lunch plate? Why should you try to eat this variety?

10. Another student at your bus stop keeps picking on you. What should you do?

11. Why should you always walk on the left side of the street?

12. Why should you remain seated when you ride on the bus or in a car?

13. Tell the class why it is necessary to listen to school patrols.

14. Why should pedestrians pay attention to street signs?

15. Aside from being mannerly, why should you not talk with your mouth full of food?

16. Name five qualities that make a good patrol.

17. Why should young children hold someone's hand while crossing a street?

18. Sometimes you are asked not to talk in the lunchroom until after you have finished eating. Why might this be so?

19. Someone on your bus is throwing things. You know who it is. Why should you tell the bus driver?

20. If you are walking or riding a bike at night, name several safety tips you can give the class.

21. Adults ask you to **walk** through a building instead of run. Why should you follow this rule?

22. Name three things that could happen if you run with a sharp object in your hand, such as a pencil or scissors.

23. Why is it important to practice emergency drills on a bus?

24. Why is it important to walk single file and quietly during a fire drill?

25. Why do drivers ask that you keep your head and arms inside the bus or car windows?

26. If you are riding home with someone else from school, why should you give your teacher a written note?

27. Why do teachers ask you to obey rules when you are having recess?

28. If the phone rings and you are home alone, why is it a good idea not to let anyone know an adult is not in the house? What could you tell the caller?

29. If you are walking to school and a stranger offers you a ride, what should you do?

30. Name several rules your school follows when your class is playing outside?

31. What should you do if you are sitting in the back of the classroom and you cannot hear?

32. If you are sitting in the back of the classroom and you cannot see the chalkboard clearly, what should you do? Why?

33. Why is it important not to goof off on the playground equipment?

# COPYCAT

I am a new student in your class.
**STOP!** Take a look at me.
I'm a lot like all the others, but
So different, as you'll see!

**CAUTION!** I am just a kid
With feelings tucked inside.
I hope you'll get to know me,
For I'm here for you to guide.

Now **GO** ahead and teach me,
Challenge me in every way—
As I go through all life's stages
When I laugh and learn and play!

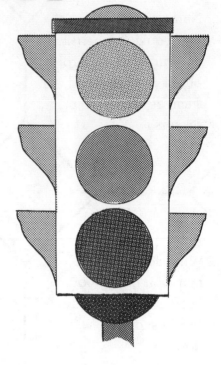

# Stop 'n Go Strips

This is a great study aid for any content area! Simply cut out this page on the solid line. Cut out the proper circle, fold on the dotted lines, and **glue the sides to each other**. This will form a pocket. Use the strips on the following page for your questions or problems, and directly below, write the answers so that questions will be self-checking. You may wish to color this before it is laminated.

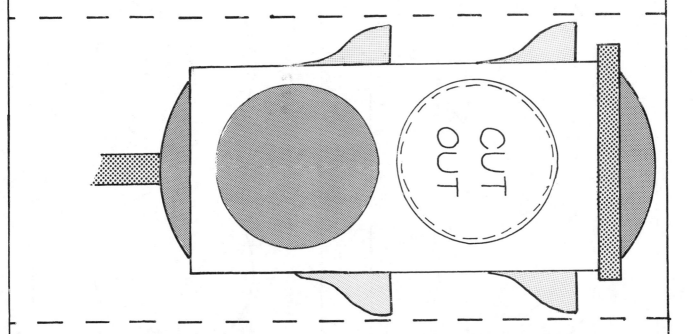

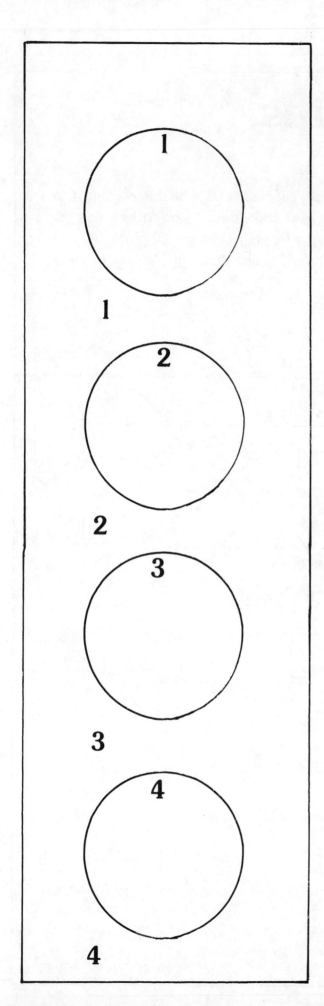

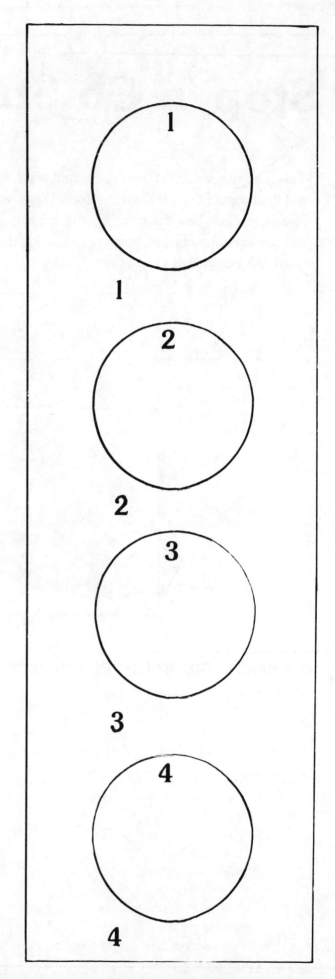

# Autumn "Tree"t

**TO CREATE THE BULLETIN BOARD, YOU WILL NEED:**

1. A large sheet of yellow background paper.
2. Patterns for the letters in the title which can be found on the following two pages.
3. A large sheet of brown butcher paper for the tree trunk and branches.
4. Various shades of green construction paper for the leaves (pattern follows).

**PRACTICAL USES:**

1. Have each student research a particular type of tree and record his findings on a leaf. Attach the leaves to the top of the tree.
2. Use the creative writing topics suggested. Place completed stories on the tree for others to read.
3. Allow students time to create poems or copy poems about trees. Display their work on the tree.
4. Ask students to read books about trees (suggestions follow in this section) and summarize their reports on leaves.
5. For variety, use multicolored leaves as autumn progresses. Let some of the leaves fall by the trunk.

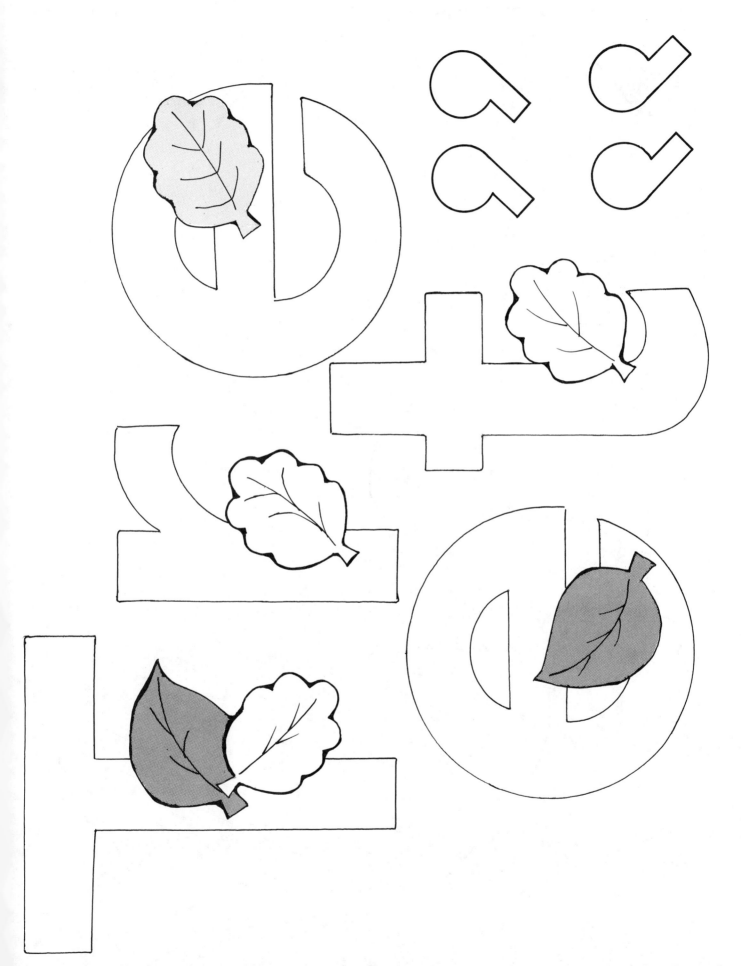

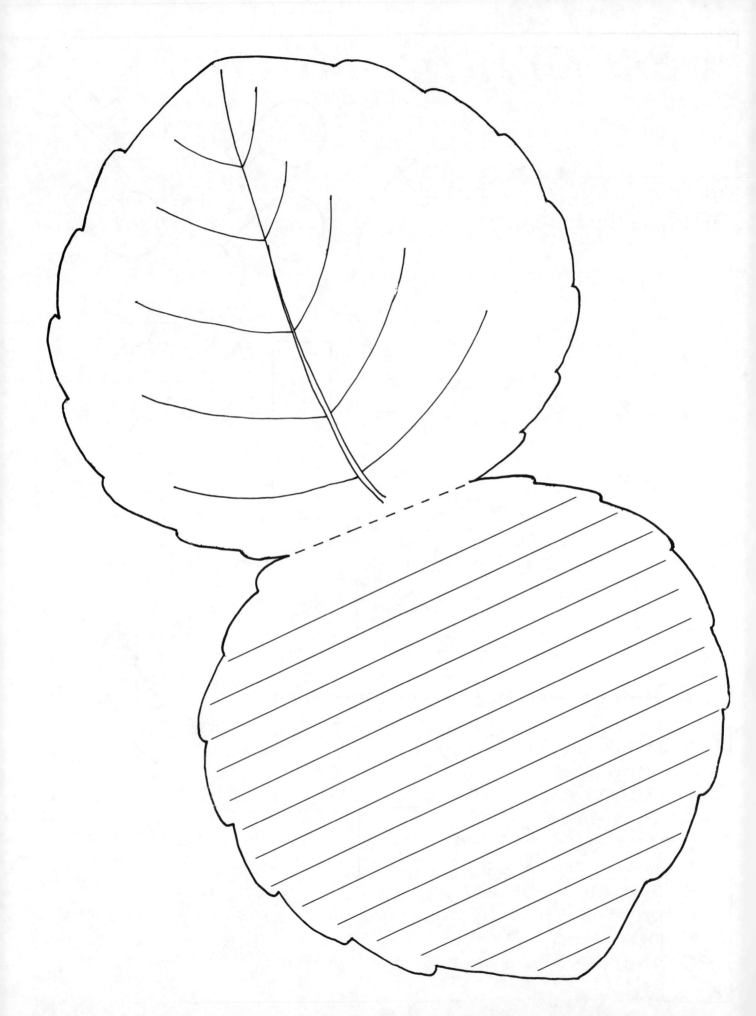

# BACKYARD BUILDERS

10 POPLAR DRIVE
SOUTH BRANCH, OHIO

| Transaction: | Customer: | | | Date: | |
|---|---|---|---|---|---|
| quantity | description | | | unit price | extended price |
| | | | | | |
| | | | | | |
| | | | subtotal | | |
| | | | sales tax | | |
| | | | TOTAL ⟶ | | |

## To Build a Tree House You Will Need:

**1  hammer** (claw)        $2.59
**2  windows**      $2.89 each
**1  sheet plywood** (3/4 in. x 4 ft. x 6 ft.)    $4.90
**1  Yale lock** $ .98
   **carpet** (4 ft. x 6 ft.)      $2.79
**1  tape measure**      $1.55
**2  hinges**    $.75 each
   **nails** (1 gross 16 penny)      $1.75
**1  saw** (hand)   $3.69
**20 boards** ( 2 in. x 4 in. x 6 ft.)      $2.87 each

49

# Which MONEY TREE makes more CENTS?

Write the sum of each tree on the trunk. Circle tree with greatest value.

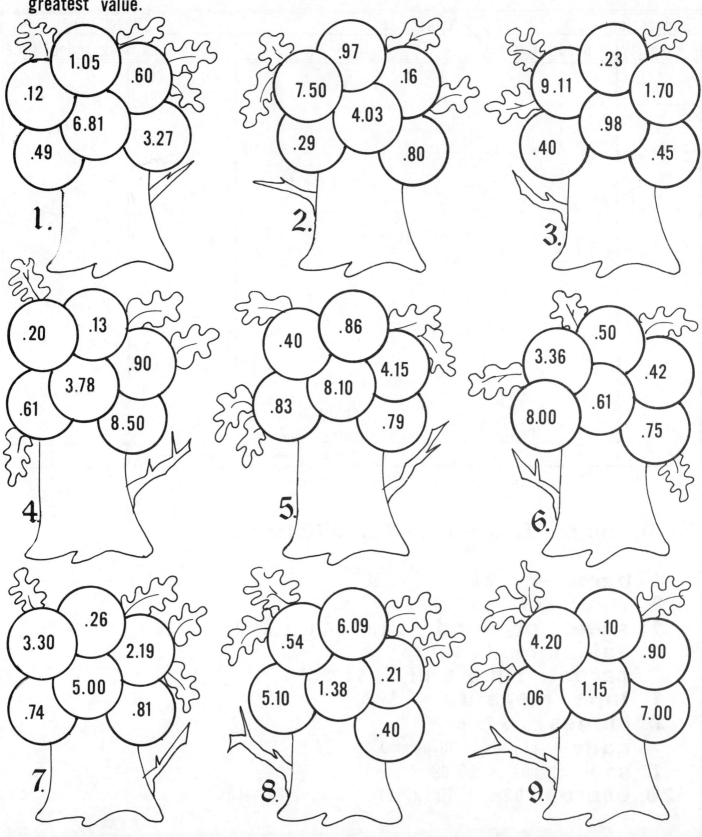

1. 1.05 .60 .12 6.81 3.27 .49

2. .97 .16 7.50 4.03 .29 .80

3. .23 9.11 1.70 .98 .40 .45

4. .20 .13 .90 3.78 .61 8.50

5. .86 .40 4.15 8.10 .83 .79

6. .50 3.36 .42 .61 8.00 .75

7. .26 3.30 2.19 5.00 .74 .81

8. 6.09 .54 .21 5.10 1.38 .40

9. .10 4.20 .90 .06 1.15 7.00

# DO LEAVES HAVE SKELETONS ?

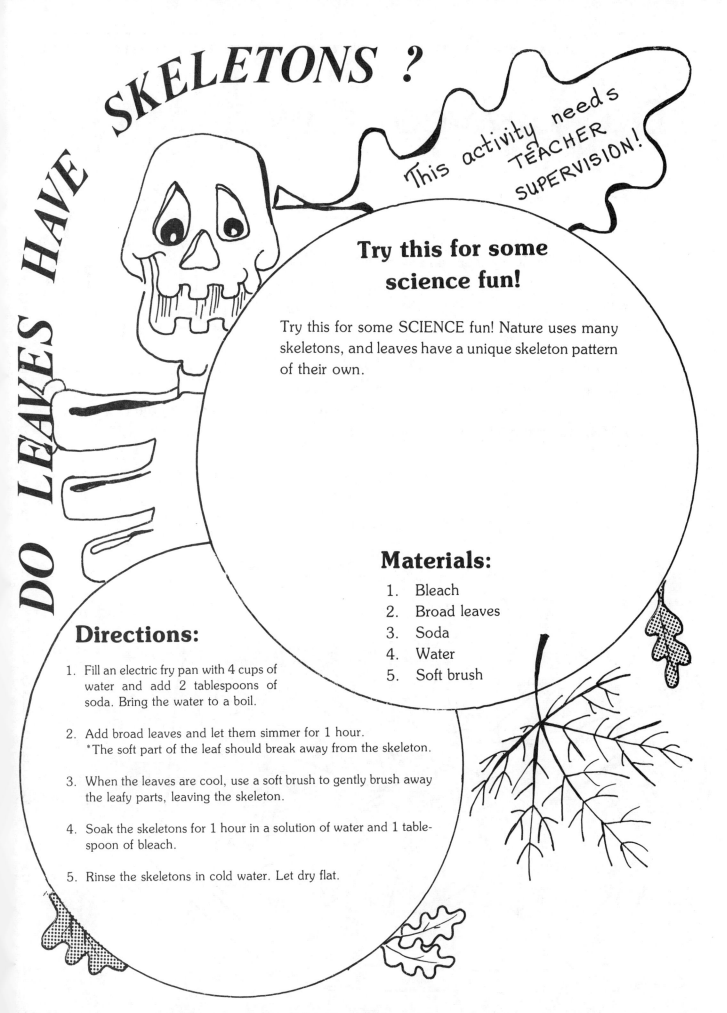

This activity needs TEACHER SUPERVISION!

## Try this for some science fun!

Try this for some SCIENCE fun! Nature uses many skeletons, and leaves have a unique skeleton pattern of their own.

## Materials:

1. Bleach
2. Broad leaves
3. Soda
4. Water
5. Soft brush

## Directions:

1. Fill an electric fry pan with 4 cups of water and add 2 tablespoons of soda. Bring the water to a boil.

2. Add broad leaves and let them simmer for 1 hour.
   *The soft part of the leaf should break away from the skeleton.

3. When the leaves are cool, use a soft brush to gently brush away the leafy parts, leaving the skeleton.

4. Soak the skeletons for 1 hour in a solution of water and 1 tablespoon of bleach.

5. Rinse the skeletons in cold water. Let dry flat.

# Do Leaves Cry?

Water moves through a tree all the time. It is drawn in by the roots and given off as water vapor by the leaves.

No, leaves don't really cry! You can prove it by doing this experiment. On a dry day, tape a plastic bag over some leaves on a tree. After a few hours, you will see moisture in the bag with the leaves in it.

Explanation: Root sap (water and minerals) flows through the stalk and into the network of veins all over the leaf. Sunlight and carbon dioxide ($CO_2$) are needed for making food. Oxygen ($O_2$) and water ($H_2O$) vapor are released in the process.

# A Spider's Tree House

When autumn comes, spiders are busy spinning. Making a web can be a lot of hard work. Observe the steps below and notice how the spider is weaving his home. After studying these steps, number them in the order the spider would make them.

Now it's your turn! Design a spider web book cover. Make a spider from colored paper to put in your web. Research spiders, collect your information and write it in your booklet. Then share it with others in your class.

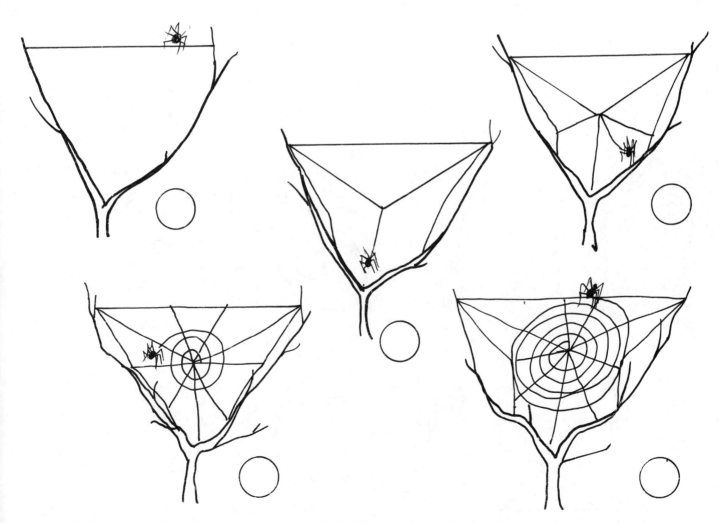

# FLOOR PLAN

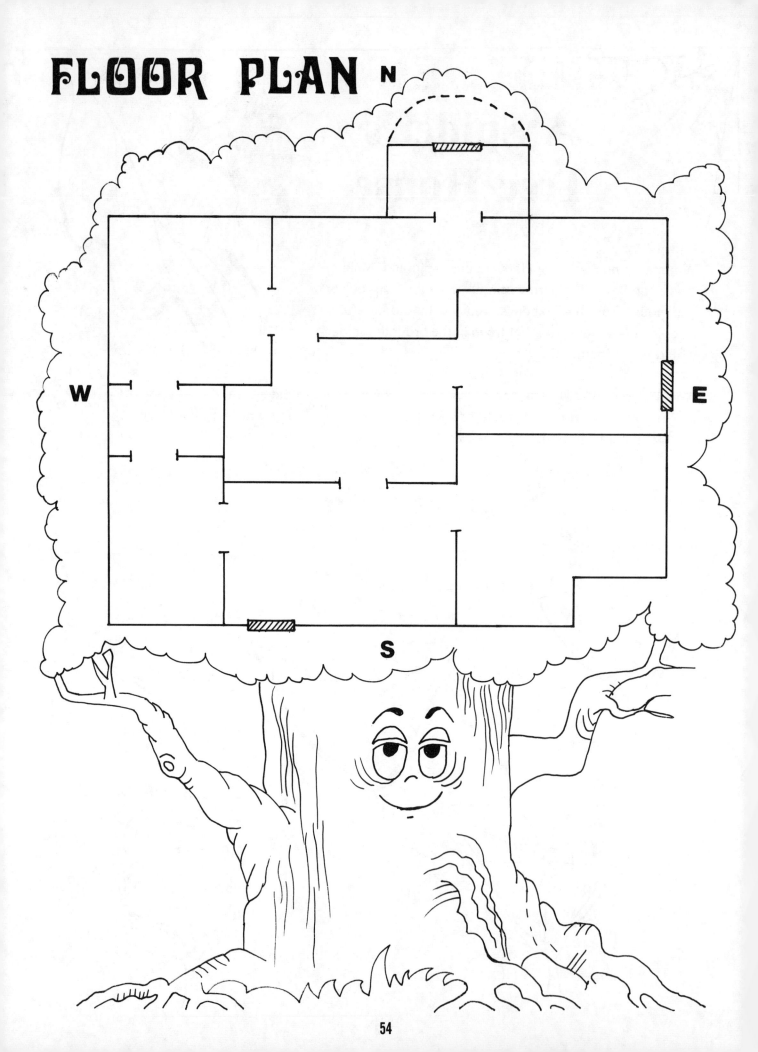

# A "TREE"MENDOUS TASK

To find the SECRET HIDING PLACE, follow these directions:

1. Place your TREE HOUSE FLOOR PLAN on your desk. Get out your crayons or markers.

2. Find a room that makes a square. Label it BEDROOM A.

3. Go directly east of Bedroom A. This is the KITCHEN. Draw a plate with silverware beside it in this room.

4. Locate a small room leading to the outside from the kitchen. Label this the LOOKOUT ROOM.

5. Notice that a DECK is attached to the Lookout Room. Color the DECK brown.

6. Find the smallest room in the house. Label this the BATHROOM.

7. Walk into the house through the door facing south. You will be in the LIVING ROOM. Label it.

8. Move eastward from the Living Room to find BEDROOM B. Write its name in the space.

9. Draw a bed in each bedroom. Color the beds blue.

10. Locate the CLUBHOUSE MEETING ROOM. You will find it just to the north of Bedroom B. Label it.

11. Between the Living Room and the Kitchen is the DINING ROOM. Write its name in that space.

12. Move westward from the Living Room to find the LIBRARY. Draw three books in this room. Color one red, one blue, and one yellow.

13. There are three doors that lead outside the tree house. Color them green.

14. In the Meeting Room, draw a round table with six chairs. Color the table and chairs yellow.

15. Draw a KEY in the Lookout Room. This will be a secret key which will unlock the SECRET HIDING PLACE. Color the key red.

16. One of the three books in your Library is not really a book. It is a treasure box shaped like a book. The key will fit the book of the same color. Place an X on your SECRET HIDING PLACE.

# NATURE'S DELIGHT

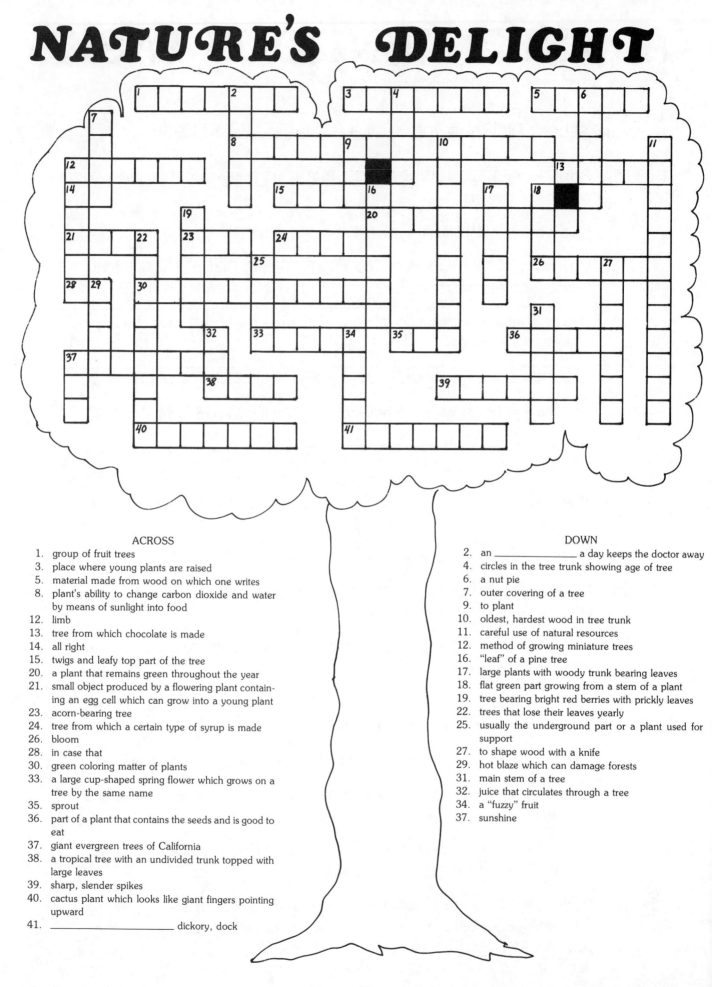

## ACROSS

1. group of fruit trees
3. place where young plants are raised
5. material made from wood on which one writes
8. plant's ability to change carbon dioxide and water by means of sunlight into food
12. limb
13. tree from which chocolate is made
14. all right
15. twigs and leafy top part of the tree
20. a plant that remains green throughout the year
21. small object produced by a flowering plant containing an egg cell which can grow into a young plant
23. acorn-bearing tree
24. tree from which a certain type of syrup is made
26. bloom
28. in case that
30. green coloring matter of plants
33. a large cup-shaped spring flower which grows on a tree by the same name
35. sprout
36. part of a plant that contains the seeds and is good to eat
37. giant evergreen trees of California
38. a tropical tree with an undivided trunk topped with large leaves
39. sharp, slender spikes
40. cactus plant which looks like giant fingers pointing upward
41. _____ dickory, dock

## DOWN

2. an _____ a day keeps the doctor away
4. circles in the tree trunk showing age of tree
6. a nut pie
7. outer covering of a tree
9. to plant
10. oldest, hardest wood in tree trunk
11. careful use of natural resources
12. method of growing miniature trees
16. "leaf" of a pine tree
17. large plants with woody trunk bearing leaves
18. flat green part growing from a stem of a plant
19. tree bearing bright red berries with prickly leaves
22. trees that lose their leaves yearly
25. usually the underground part or a plant used for support
27. to shape wood with a knife
29. hot blaze which can damage forests
31. main stem of a tree
32. juice that circulates through a tree
34. a "fuzzy" fruit
37. sunshine

# A FUN "TREE"T

If I were a tree I'd

like to be a _____

because _____

_____

_____

_____

```
D I G H P A U H S O J
W S Y C A M O R E H B
O E R E L A N N Q S I
S E A E M P O P L A R
U D E B X L I Z A X C
T A P P L E Z L L S H
P I H C A E P W U E E
Y O N J G I F A M T R
L U A W I E X L F A R
A Q C H N Y O N A O Y
C E E I G C G U E C Q
U S P Z K V U T L O P
E N Y R O K C I H C R
```

Name several PRODUCTS we
get from trees.

_____

_____

_____

_____

The PARTS of a TREE are:

_____

_____

_____

Kinds of Trees:

1. _____
2. _____
3. _____
4. _____
5. _____
6. _____
7. _____
8. _____
9. _____
10. _____
11. _____
12. _____
13. _____
14. _____

57

# CREATIVE WRITING IDEAS FOR
# AUTUMN AUTHORS

1. My Best Friend
2. My Favorite Sport
3. If I Could Be Someone Else, I'd Choose to Be _____
4. The Worst Day I Ever Had
5. The Best Surprise
6. One Scary Night
7. My Most Embarrassing Moment
8. My Dream Vacation
9. How My Family Celebrates _____(holiday)
10. My Hobby
11. My Favorite TV Show
12. Summer Camp
13. My Favorite Season of the Year
14. My Pet
15. My Best Vacation I Ever Had
16. The Greatest Invention
17. How To (make or do something)
18. My Goals
19. The Person Who Has Had the Greatest Influence on Me
20. What I Like About School
21. My Favorite Holiday
22. My Secret Place
23. The Best Present I Ever Received
24. Me—the Hero
25. My State/Province
26. My _____ Collection
27. My Family
28. The Greatest Experience I Ever Had
29. My Room
30. I Am Happiest When _____

**NOTE:** Each topic could be written on a leaf and displayed on the bulletin board with the title "Autumn Authors." Completed stories written on leaves can also be added!

# Can You "BeLeaf" This Is SPELLING?

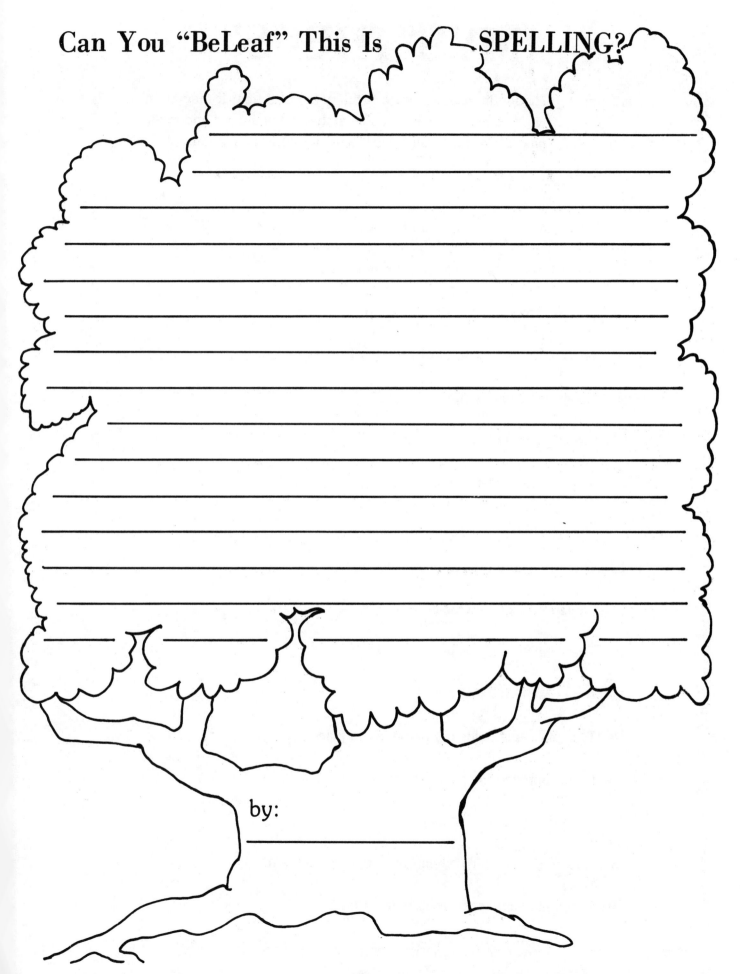

by:

# MYS "TREES"

Directions: Hidden in each sentence is the name of a tree. It may be in one word completely, or it may be at the end of a word and the beginning of the next. CIRCLE the name of the tree when you find it!

1. I watched as Penny ran down the street.

2. Elmer dropped his pencil on the floor.

3. The driver of the car obeyed the policeman.

4. That man goes to the store every day!

5. Early in the spring you can hear the frogs croaking.

6. My sister's name is Ashley.

7. Did you see the map Leslie drew?

8. My pal makes friends easily.

9. Will owes me a dollar.

10. That pop Larry brought is on the table.

11. I love to eat gummy bears.

12. That bee chased me around the yard.

13. A pea rarely is eaten raw.

14. That pin easily holds my name tag in place.

15. Camp horrified me for a few days!

16. Are those plants ever green?

17. Rub berries carefully when you are washing them.

18. A whistling tea kettle really bothers me.

60

# BOOK REPORT

by : _____

Plot :
_____
_____
_____
_____
_____
_____
_____
_____
_____
_____
_____

Best Part :
_____
_____
_____
_____
_____
_____
_____
_____

Title : _____

Author : _____

Setting : _____

Characters : _____
_____
_____

Pages : _____

# RAKE in the RHYMES

Read the poem below. On the lines following, write each italicized word with the correct rhyme. Each list has been started for you.

*There* is a big *tree* in *my yard*,
To climb *it* isn't very *hard*.
I *take* my arms and reach up *high*
And put my feet on a branch *nearby*.
I pull myself up just a *little*,
Before *you* know it I'm up in the *middle*.
I always *try to be* careful, *too*,
*Especially when* the top comes *into view*.
I have a spot *where* I always *sit*.
And I can't hear my folks a *bit*!
I climb *way* up and spend the *day*—
I read, I rest, eat lunch and *play*.
And sometimes when I hear MOM *call*
I just don't answer her at *all*.
For if I *do she'll make me* come in
And *then* she'll know just where I've *been*!

1.  there _____
2.  _____
3.  little _____
4.  _____
5.  it _____
6.  _____
7.  _____
8.  way _____
9.  _____
10. _____

11. tree _____
12. _____
13. _____
14. _____
15. _____
16. you _____
17. _____
18. _____
19. _____
20. _____
21. _____

22. my _____
23. _____
24. _____
25. _____
26. _____
27. when _____
28. _____
29. _____
30. call _____
31. _____

32. yard _____
33. _____
34. take _____
35. _____

# BRANCHING OUT....

These books will provide students with a wealth of knowledge, a resource for learning, and a pleasure for reading!

Blocksma, Mary. *Apple Tree! Apple Tree!* Chicago: Childrens Press, 1983.

Blough, Glenn O. *Christmas Trees and How They Grow*. New York: McGraw-Hill, 1961.

_____. *Lookout of the Forest; A Conservation Story*. New York: McGraw-Hill, 1955.

Boulton, Carolyn. *Trees*. New York: Franklin Watts, 1984.

Brandt, Keith. *Discovering Trees*. Troll Associates, 1982.

Bulla, Clyde Robert. *A Tree Is a Plant*. New York: Thomas Y. Crowell Co., 1960.

Cormack, M.B. *The First Book of Trees*. New York: Franklin Watts, 1951.

Littledale, Freya. *The Magic Plum Tree*. New York: Crown Pub., Inc., 1981.

O'Brien, Thomas M. *To Know a Tree*. New York: Holt, 1963.

Oppenheim, Joanne. *Have You Seen Trees?* New York: William R. Scott, 1967.

Podendorf, Illa. *The True Book of Trees*. Chicago: Childrens Press, 1954.

Poulet, Virginia. *Blue Bug Finds a Friend*. Chicago: Childrens Press, 1977.

*Silverstein, Shel. *The Giving Tree*. Harper & Row, 1964.

Udry, Janice May. *A Tree Is Nice*. Harper & Row, 1956.

Watts, May Theilgaard. *The Doubleday First Guide to Trees*. Doubleday, 1964.

Webber, Irma E. *Thanks to Trees*. New York: William R. Scott, 1952.

York, Carol Beach. *The Tree House Mystery*. New York: Coward, McCann, and Geoghegan, Inc., 1973.

*A book your students will want to hear you read again and again!

# Delightful "Bitefull"

**TO CREATE THE BULLETIN BOARD, YOU WILL NEED:**
1. A large sheet of light-green background paper.
2. Patterns for the letters in the title which can be found on the following three pages.
3. Patterns for the candy apples which can be made from construction paper (page 69). Laminate the "topping" or cover it with cellophane to produce the "candy" effect.
4. Directions for making candy apples which can be found on the bags of Kraft caramels. Use your own recipe if you prefer.

**PRACTICAL USES:**
1. Use the bulletin board to kick off an afternoon of fun. Have students make small candy apples to display on the bulletin board. Have them copy in their best handwriting the recipe for making candy apples. Make the candy apples with your class and follow the activity with a language experience.
2. Use the bulletin board to supplement classroom concepts station work. A manipulative center for contractions is included in this section.

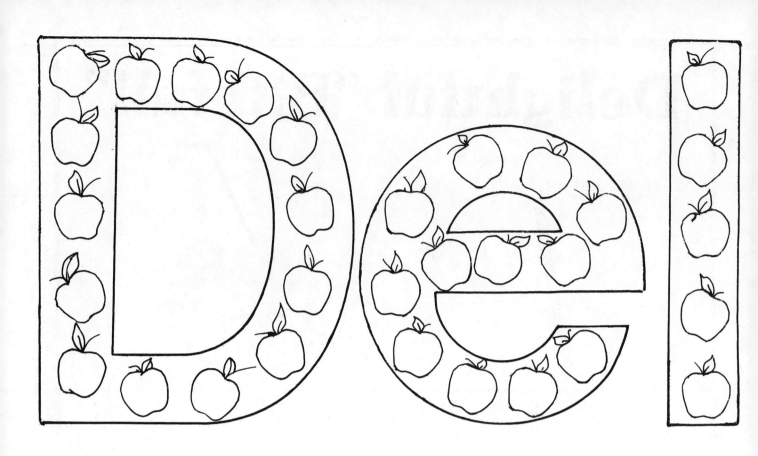

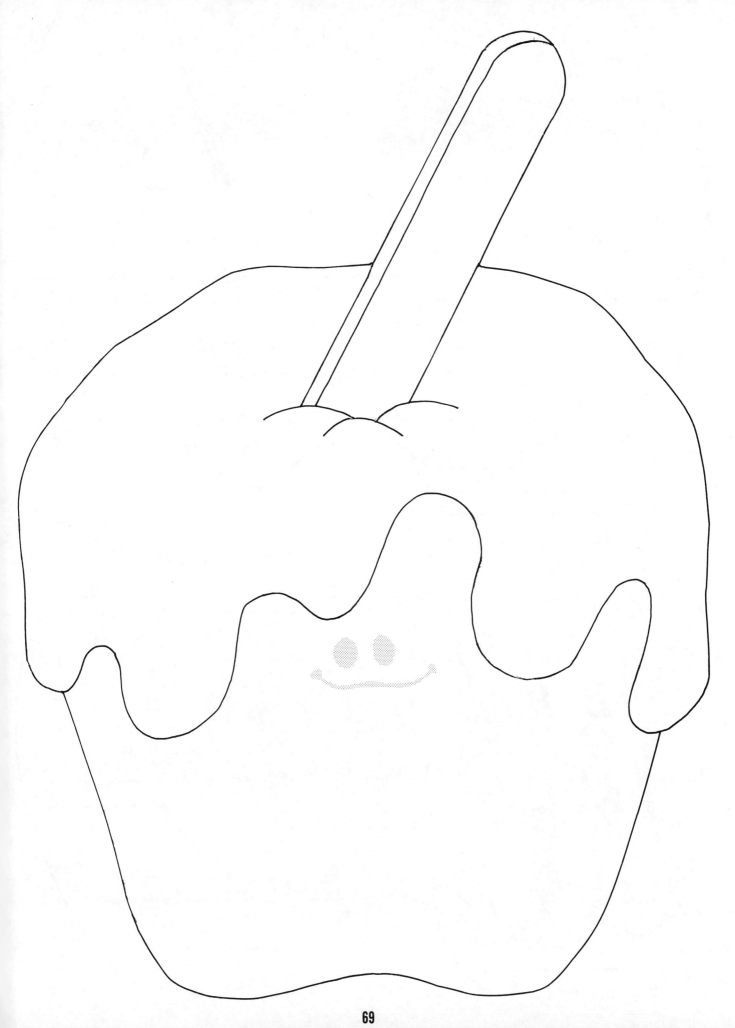

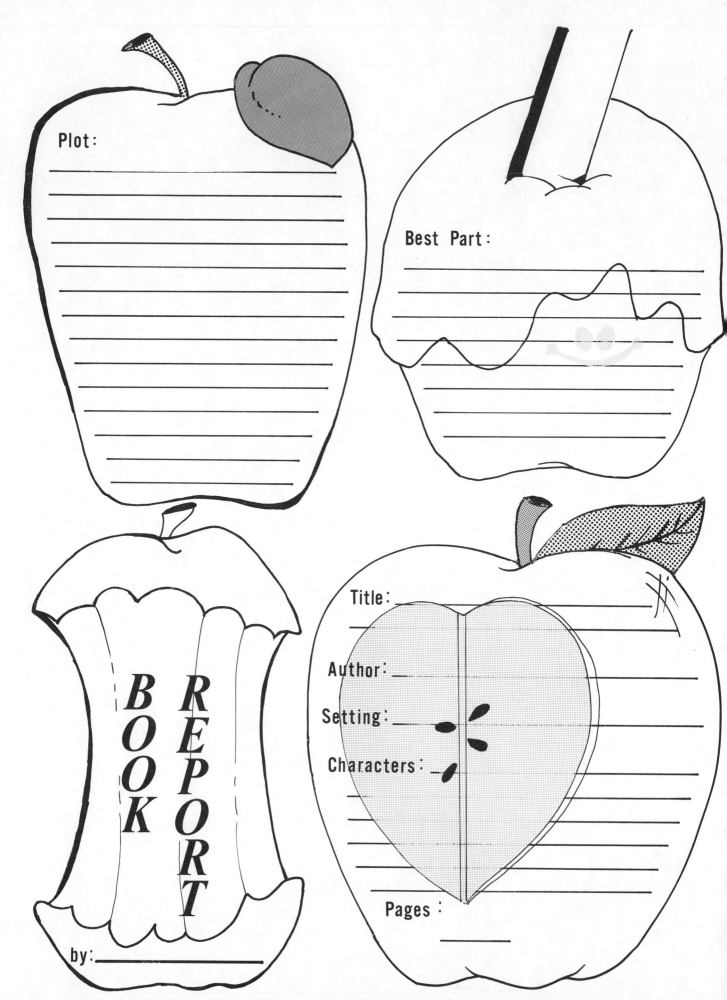

Plot:

Best Part:

BOOK REPORT

by:

Title:

Author:

Setting:

Characters:

Pages:

# *Sticky Contractions*
## LANGUAGE ARTS

Your students will love this individual or partner activity! Cut out both the picture and the title strip on this page. Glue them to the front of a sturdy envelope. Cut out the apples/toppings found on the following pages. Write the correct answers on the backs of the apples. Laminate them before placing them in the envelope. Let students work alone or with a friend to reinforce the skill of writing contractions. A blank page has been added for your convenience. This activity can be used for most content areas. Examples: multiplication facts match, spelling word/definition match, etc.

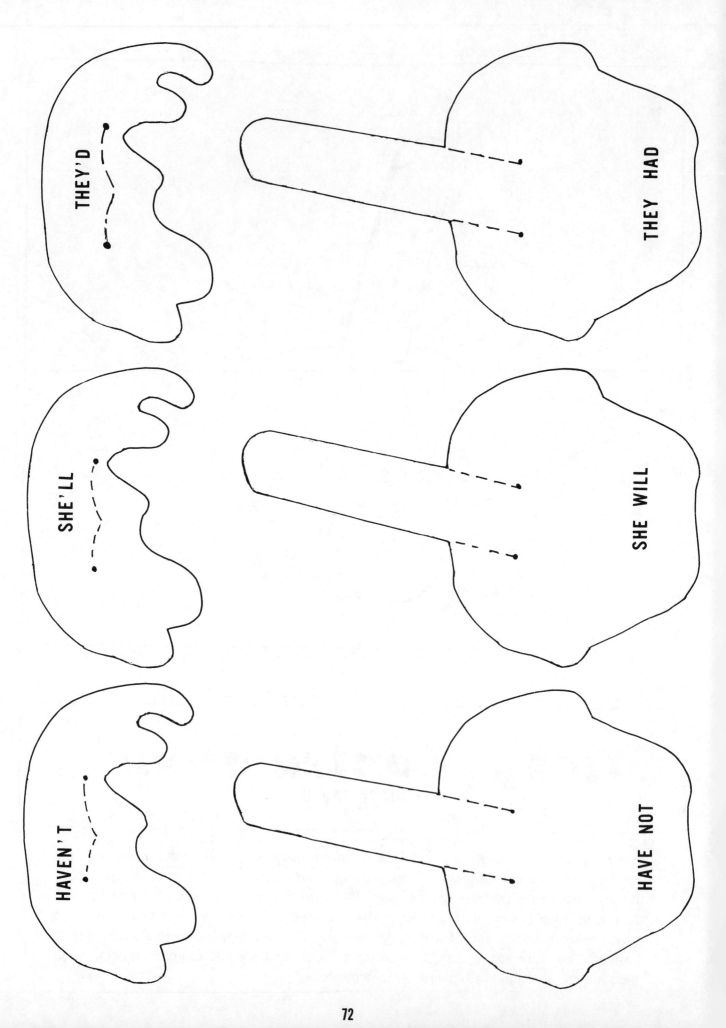

THEY'D

THEY HAD

SHE'LL

SHE WILL

HAVEN'T

HAVE NOT

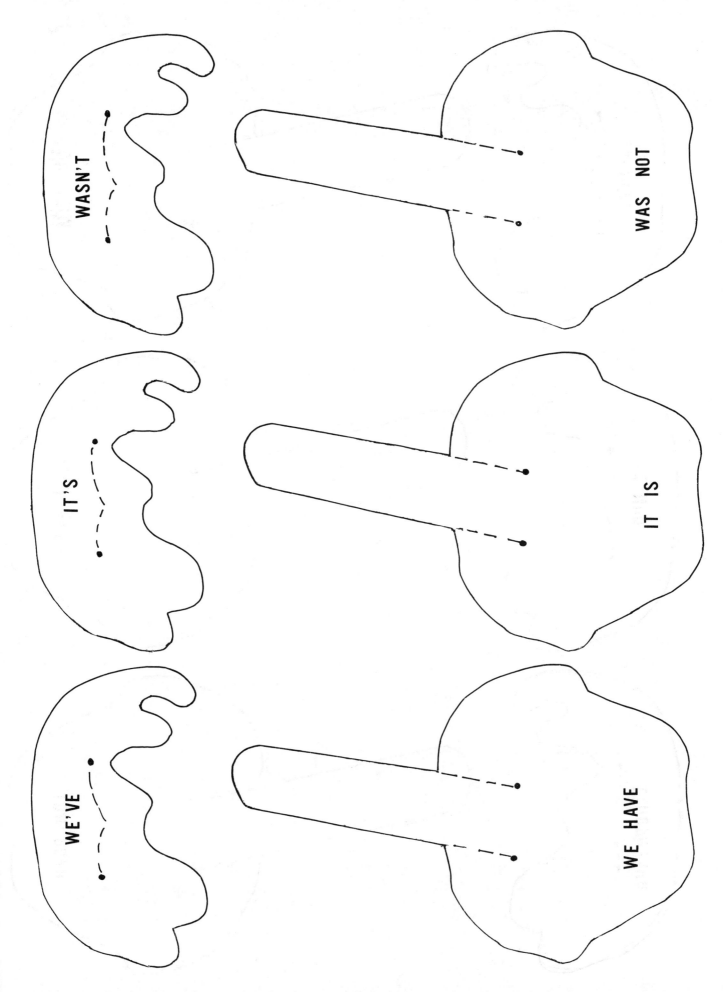

WASN'T

WAS NOT

IT'S

IT IS

WE'VE

WE HAVE

73

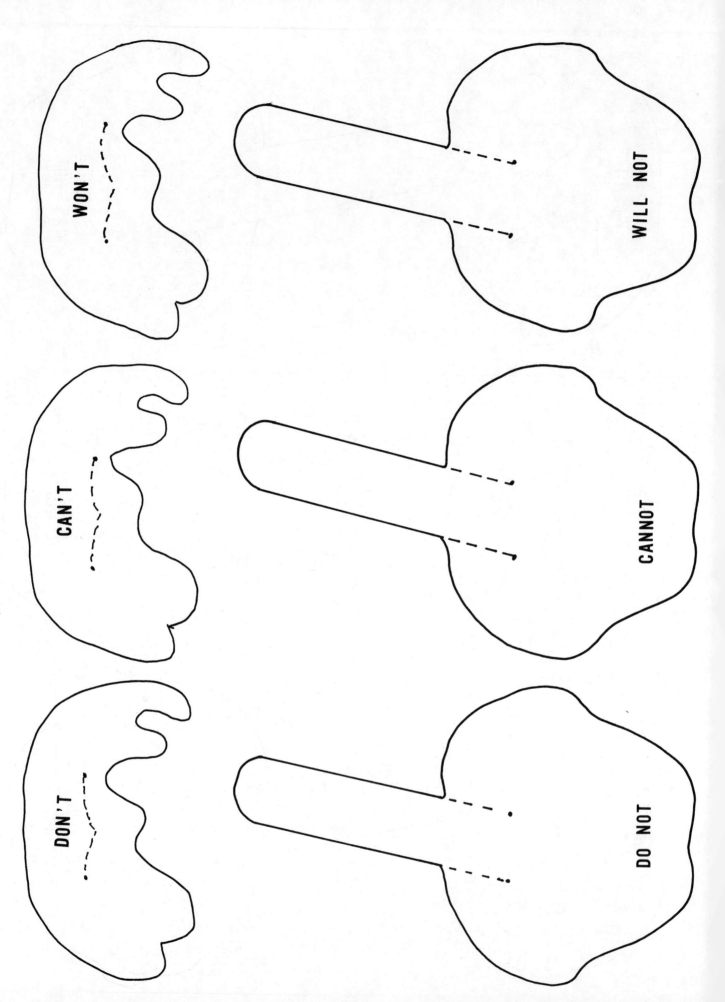

WON'T

WILL NOT

CAN'T

CANNOT

DON'T

DO NOT

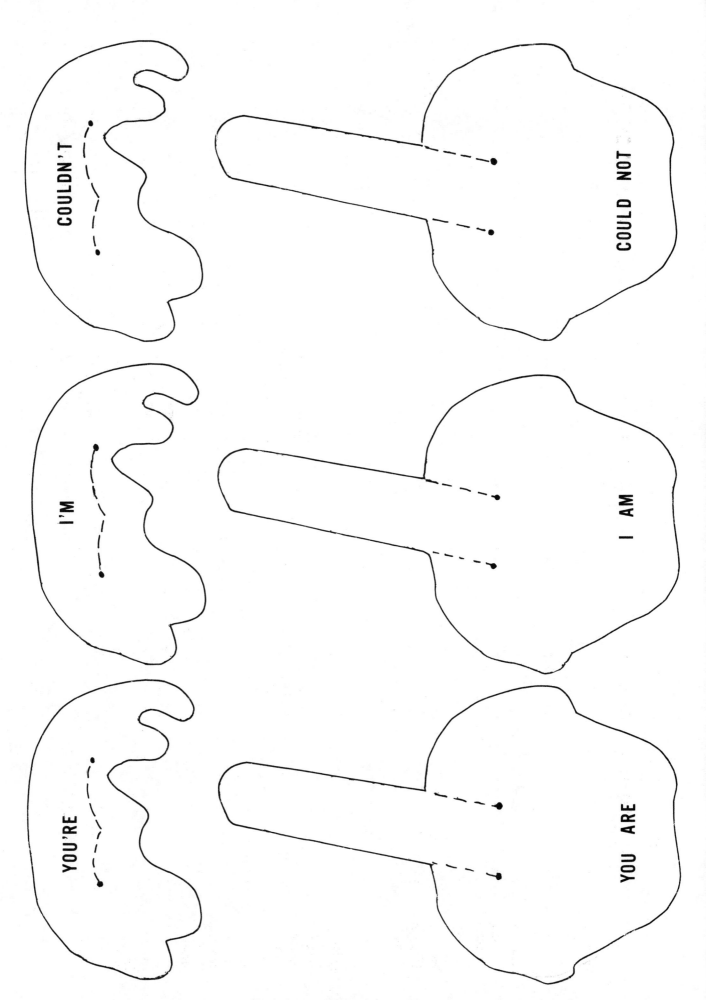

COULDN'T

COULD NOT

I'M

I AM

YOU'RE

YOU ARE

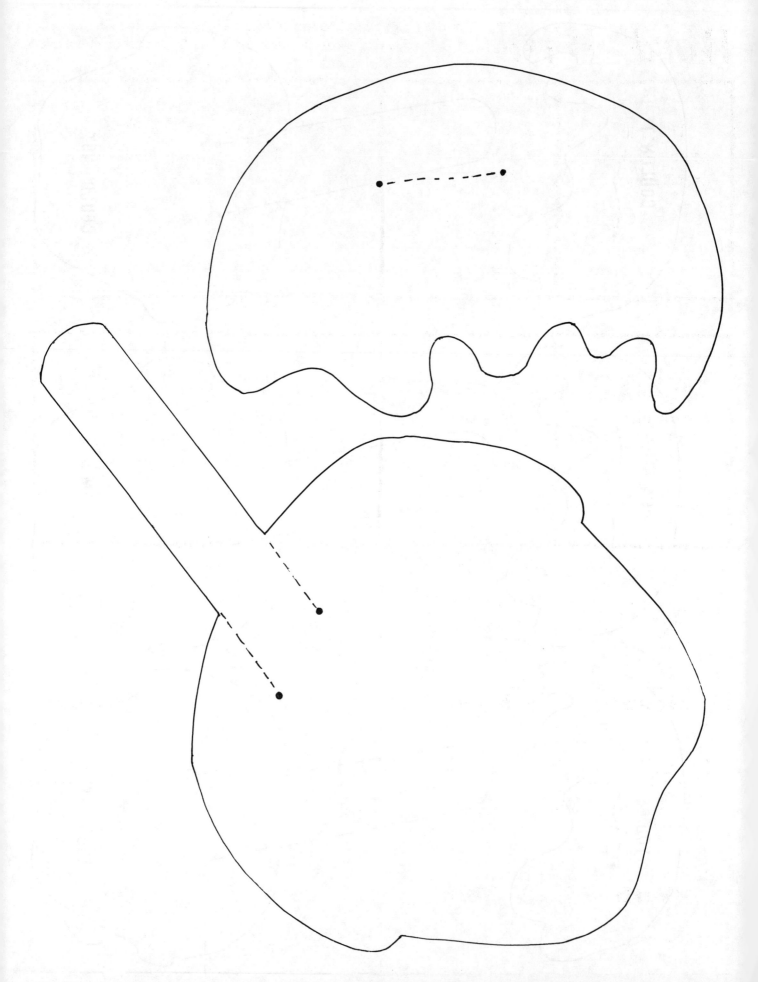

# Word Wise

Cut apart the apples below along the dotted lines. Read the sentences and glue an apple to correctly label each italized word.

1. The little puppy chewed on his *bone*.

2. We *went* on a hayride last Saturday.

3. I *left* my jacket on the fence at the park.

4. Those *pumpkins* will make delicious pies.

5. My sister *is* a cheerleader.

6. We *climbed* to the top of the Statue of Liberty.

7. Sometimes Mom and I go to the *Mall*.

8. The only *characters* in my story were a witch and a cat.

**Noun**    **Noun**    **Noun**    **Noun**

**Verb**    **Verb**    **Verb**    **Verb**

# "STICK" to Your Topic

When you write a paragraph, all of the sentences should provide details about the main idea. Remember to always "STICK TO YOUR TOPIC."

Read the following paragraphs. Cross out the sentence in each paragraph that does not belong. Now turn your paper over on the back and write a paragraph of your own!

1. One night my friends and I decided to sleep outside in our tent. We got our sleeping bags, radio, and some food. I watched TV. We said "Good night to Mom and then carried our things out to the tent. It was dark and pretty scary.

2. My favorite season of the year is autumn. The leaves begin to fall and I love to rake them into a pile. Sometimes I help Dad rake them into bags. We put up a new fence last year. My family goes on picnics and takes walks through the crunchy leaves. Autumn is a fun time for me.

3. Last summer Dad taught me how to dive. He reminded me often to keep my head down and my knees bent as I went headfirst into the water. The lifeguard blew her whistle. We practiced diving over and over again. Now I can dive by myself.

4. Whenever I have free time I love to read. My little brother can't read very well. I enjoy all kinds of books, but my favorite stories are mysteries.

5. I love to go to Grandma's house. She always lets me help her bake. Uncle Joe lives nearby. She lets me ride Banjo, the new pony. Sometimes Grandma even rides with me!

6. My gym teacher just taught my class how to play basketball. I can play soccer, too. We learned the rules and then we practiced dribbling. Tomorrow he will show us how to pass and shoot.

This autumn decoration is sure to capture the looks of all who see it. Title it "A Great Class, Starring . . ."

Make a large oaktag pattern of the moon. Color it before it is laminated. Attach it to your classroom door.

Give each child a copy of the star pattern found on the following page. Ask him to write on the star the "things that make me shine!" (strengths) Then ask him to sign his name, cut out his star, and display it on the door. (Vary the assignment, if you like, to meet the needs of your class.)

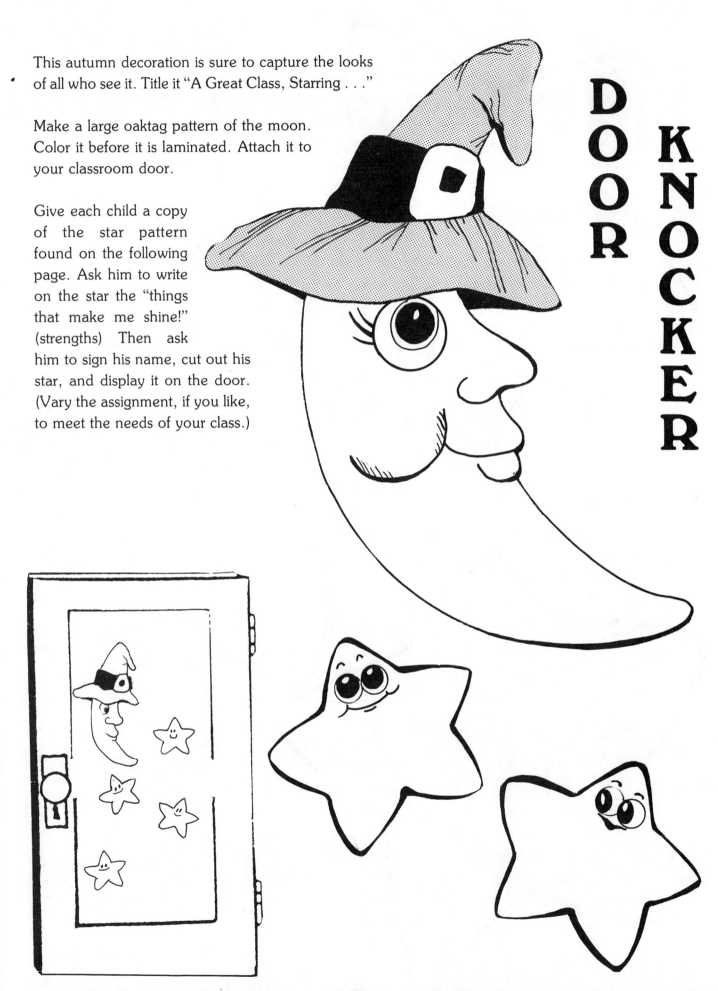

DOOR KNOCKER

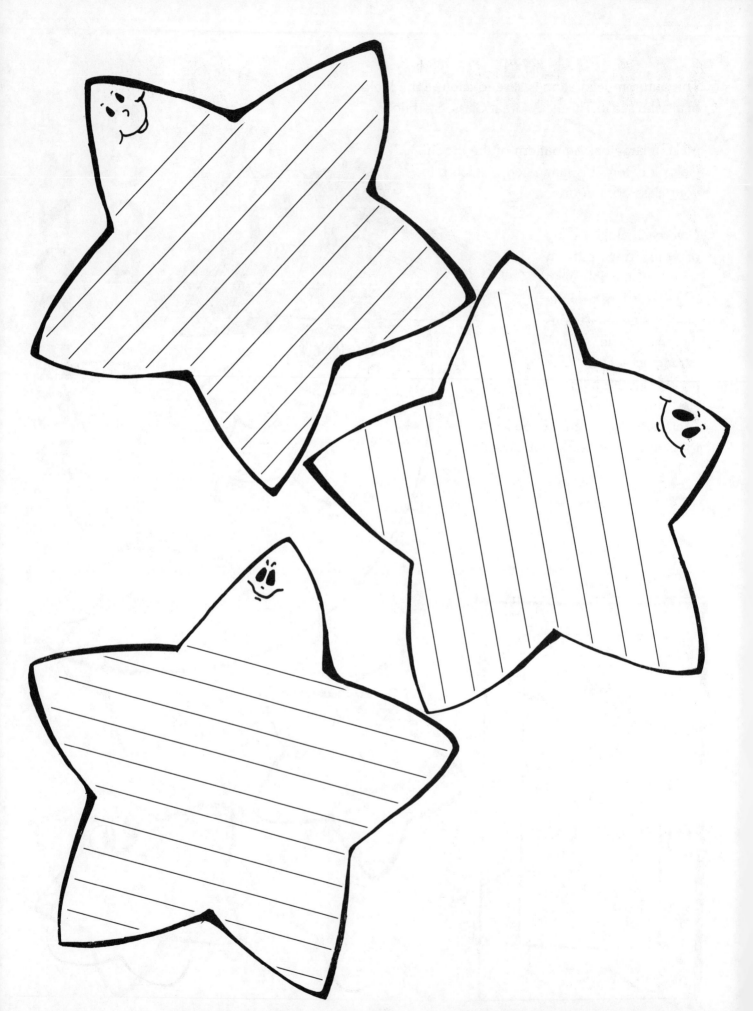

# ALL-STAR ADDITION

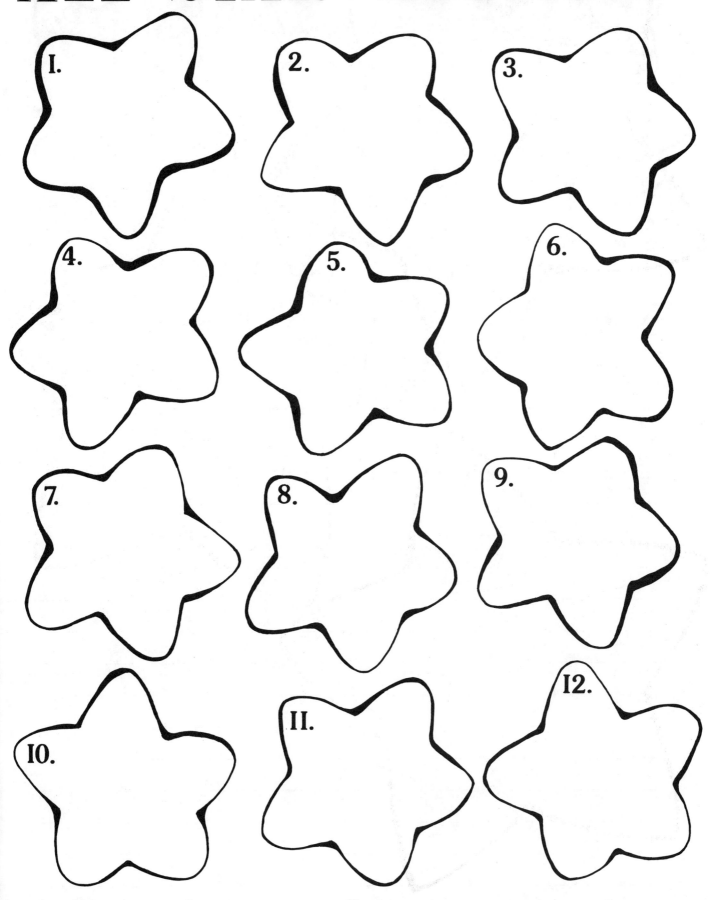

1.

2.

3.

4.

5.

6.

7.

8.

9.

10.

11.

12.

# COPYCAT

## IF

If you'll be my shining star,
I'll be your harvest moon.
Together we will work and play
From morn 'till afternoon!

If you'll let your star twinkle,
I'll shine my beam on you.
I'll share a little part of me;
You can teach me something new!

If you'll try to be the best,
Take pride in everything—
I will wish you happiness
In all that life can bring!

_____

_____

_____

_____

_____

_____

_____

_____

_____

_____

_____

_____

_____

## TO CREATE THE BULLETIN BOARD, YOU WILL NEED:

1. A large sheet of yellow background paper.
2. Patterns for the letters in the title which can be found on the following three pages.
3. Brown butcher paper or poster paper for the wagon and the wheel.
4. Large sheet of poster paper for the scarecrow. For a 3-D effect, use a wooden yard-stick for the body, a paper plate for the head, fringed yellow crepe paper or yarn for the hair and straw. Add a real jacket and hat if possible.
5. Orange construction paper for the pumpkins (patterns follow).

## PRACTICAL USES:

1. Honor students with a Great Pumpkin Award. Attach their pictures to the award and place pumpkins on the wagon.
2. Display excellent handwriting papers, spelling, English papers, etc., by asking students to complete their work on the lined pumpkins.
3. Use the wagon to display extra credit projects from any content area.
4. Place school pictures or candid shots of your students doing various activities on the pumpkins.

# Great Pumpkin Award

_____

### IS  HONORED  ON

THIS _____ DAY  OF _____

FOR _____

_____

**Presenter**

**1** Debbie invited 32 students in her class to a Halloween party. Only 19 came. How many students missed the party?

**2** Last Saturday my friends and I picked pumpkins. Sandy picked 24, Kim picked 18, Melissa picked 17, and I picked 21. How many pumpkins did we pick in all?

**3** Ronnie is reading a book of ghost stories. There are 148 pages in the book. If he is on page 96, how many more pages does he have left to read?

**4** Mom bought 2 bags of Halloween candy. If there are 102 pieces in one bag and 59 in the other, how many pieces does she have?

**5** Jeremy had $15.00 to buy a Halloween costume. If his mask cost $3.95 and his costume was $8.99, how much did he spend?_____ How much change did he receive?_____

**6** My class went on a hayride. There were 6 adults, 18 boys, and 14 girls. How many people went on the hayride?

**AS EASY AS PIE**

# STRIPS OF FUN!

Children love PUZZLES! Here is a strip of nine interlocking pumpkins. Make each strip a different color so they will be easy to sort. The puzzle will be self-checking since the pieces will fit together properly. Here are a few interesting ways to use them in your classroom.

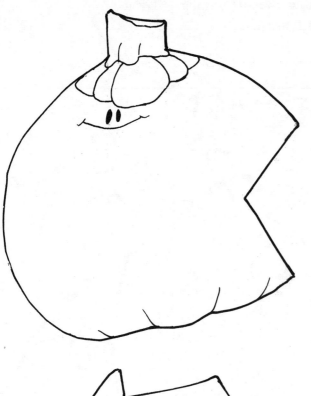

1. SENTENCE STRIPS—Write a word on each pumpkin. When the pumpkins are fit together properly they will make a complete sentence. If you choose, have students copy the sentences on paper using correct capitalization and punctuation.
2. MATH STRIPS—Write a number on each pumpkin. Ask students to add or to multiply the complete strip of numbers.
3. LANGUAGE ARTS—Write a brief direction on each pumpkin. Let students put the strips in the correct sequence. When completed, the puzzle will have organized directions for making something. Example: How to make a peanut butter and jelly sandwich.
4. An activity of YOUR CHOICE!

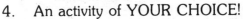

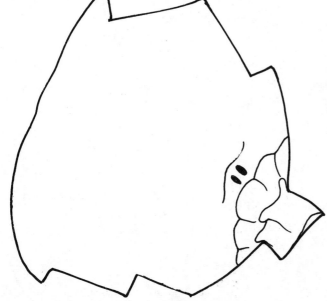

# HARVEST TIME

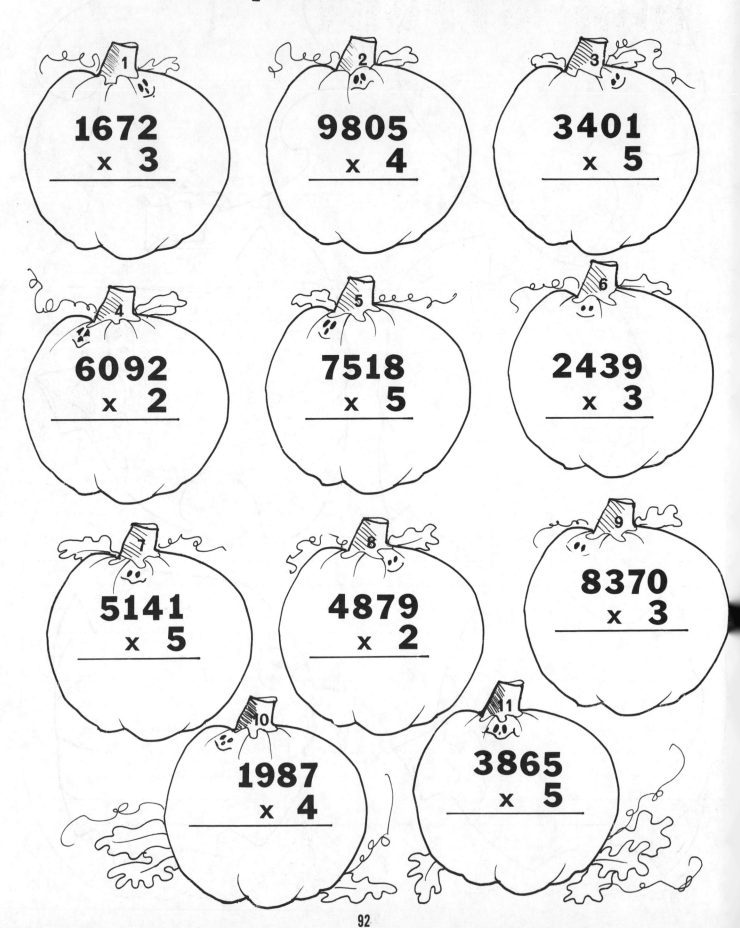

1. 1672 × 3

2. 9805 × 4

3. 3401 × 5

4. 6092 × 2

5. 7518 × 5

6. 2439 × 3

7. 5141 × 5

8. 4879 × 2

9. 8370 × 3

10. 1987 × 4

11. 3865 × 5

# BOOK REPORT

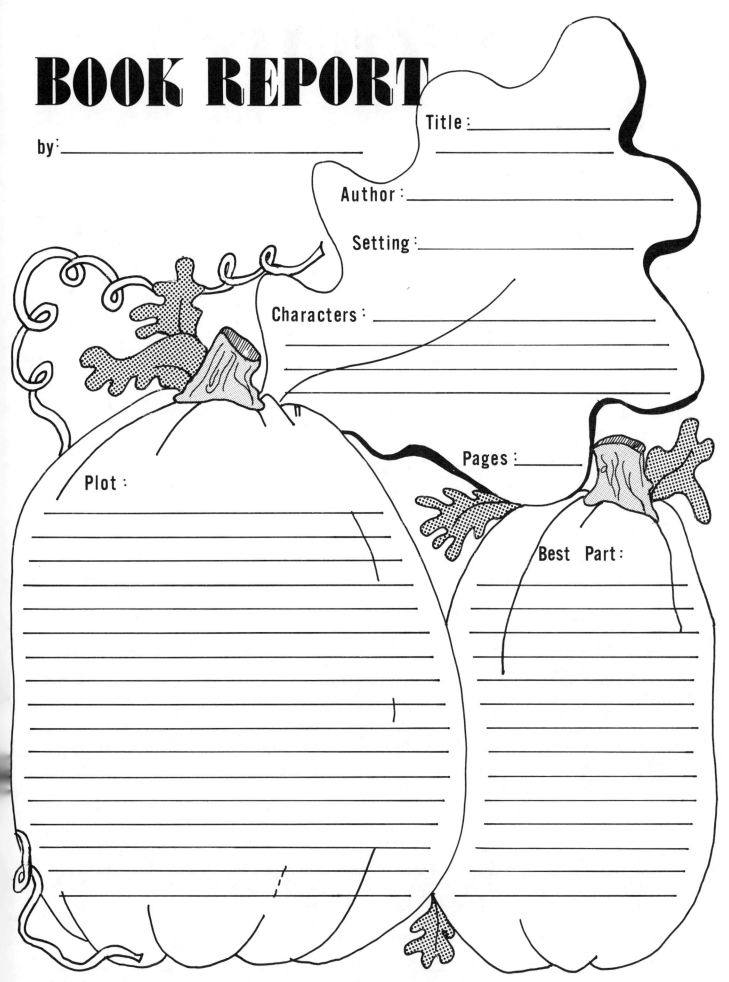

by:_____

Title:_____
_____

Author:_____

Setting:_____

Characters:_____
_____
_____

Plot:
_____
_____
_____
_____
_____
_____
_____
_____
_____
_____
_____

Pages:_____

Best Part:
_____
_____
_____
_____
_____
_____

# COPYCAT

When I do my work in school,
    I try my very best.
Yet sometimes when I study hard
    I still don't pass my test!

Some classes I like very much,
    So I get my work done.
The others are more difficult,
    And just don't seem as fun!

But I will try with all my heart
    To keep my work from laggin',
And then you'll see my work someday
    Upon the BRAGGIN' WAGON.

# Teepee Trivia

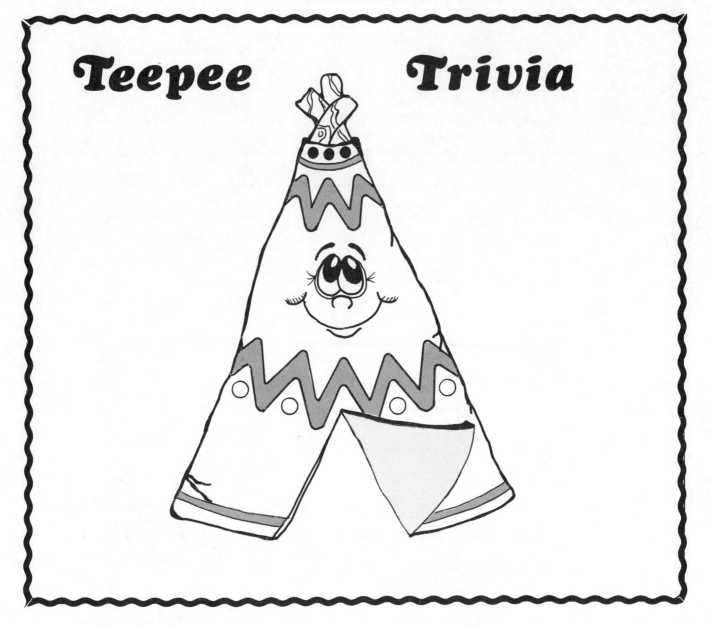

**TO CREATE THE BULLETIN BOARD, YOU WILL NEED:**

1. A large sheet of light-blue background paper.
2. Patterns for the letters in the title which can be found on the following two pages.
3. A large teepee made from poster paper and colored. Brown butcher paper could also be used.
4. Pattern of the teepee for each child to be made from oaktag or construction paper (page 99). Fold it for a 3-D effect before attaching to the bulletin board.

**PRACTICAL USES:**

1. Use the bulletin board to stimulate interest in the study of Indians. Attach pictures around the teepee in the center for discussion.
2. Attach student projects to the bulletin board for display.
3. Use the bulletin board as a center where the research cards are kept. Or let students create Indian trivia work sheets for the class and place them in envelopes on the bulletin board.

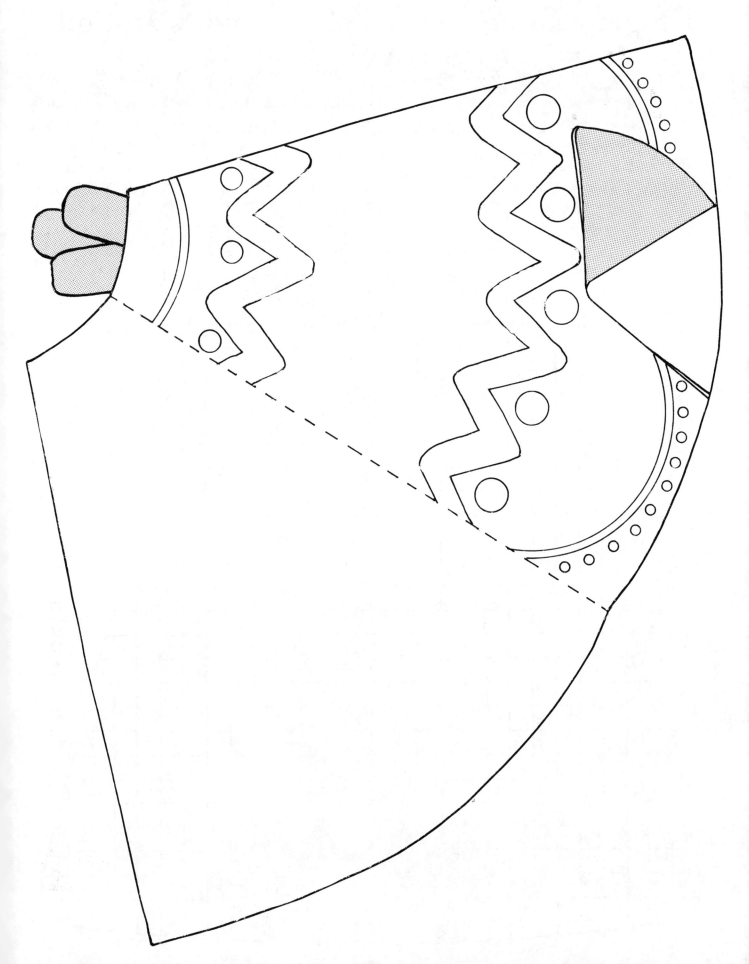

# Happy Hunting Ground

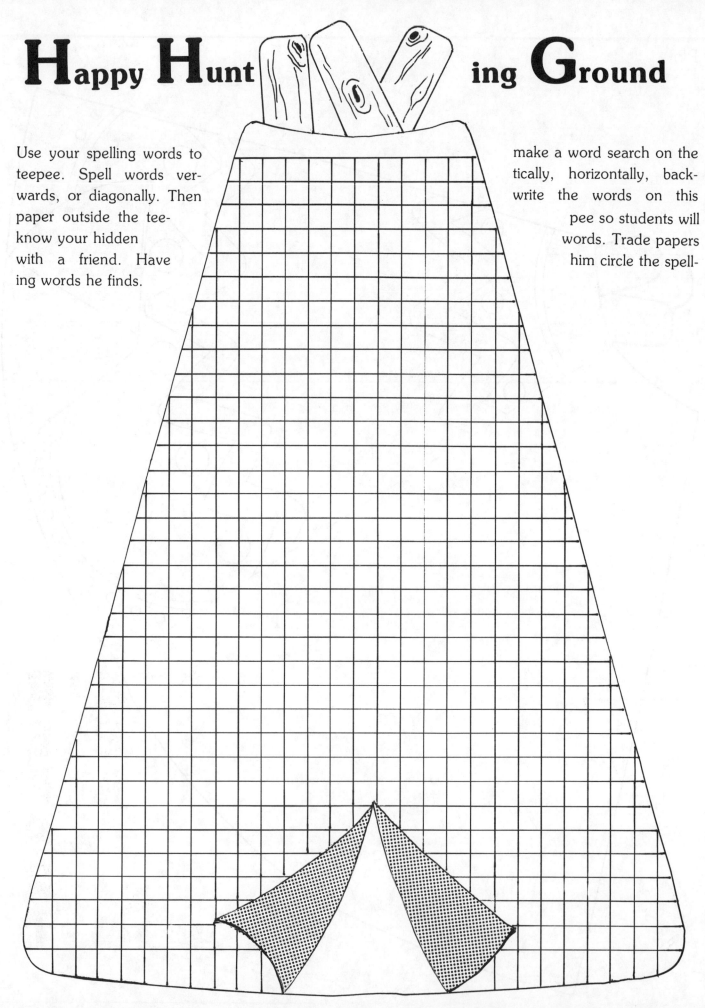

Use your spelling words to teepee. Spell words ver- wards, or diagonally. Then paper outside the tee- know your hidden with a friend. Have ing words he finds.

make a word search on the tically, horizontally, back- write the words on this pee so students will words. Trade papers him circle the spell-

Plot:

_____

_____

_____

_____

_____

_____

_____

_____

_____

_____

_____

_____

_____

_____

_____

_____

_____

_____

_____

_____

_____

_____

Title: _____

_____

Author: _____

Setting: _____

Characters: _____

_____

_____

_____

_____

Pages: _____

Best Part:

_____

_____

_____

_____

_____

_____

_____

_____

_____

_____

by: _____

BOOK REPORT

101

# READY, SET, RESEARCH

SOCIAL STUDIES

Here is a terrific way to individualize class projects and to motivate the students. Get a sturdy envelope. Cut out both the picture and the title strip on this page and glue them on the front of the envelope. Cut out the social studies cards found on the following pages. Laminate them before placing them inside the envelope. Let students choose a card, complete the activity, and then return the card to the envelope. You may wish to have each student complete a certain number of projects. You may also wish to delete or to expand the activities. Substitute ideas of your own to suit the needs of your classroom.

1. Pretend that you are an Indian chief. List ten qualities that make you a good leader for your tribe. Rank them from 1-10, with 1 being the most important.

2. Indians performed dances for various reasons—for rain, for a good crop, for preparation for war, etc. Make up an Indian dance, describe its purpose, and teach it to your class.

3. Buffalo were very important to the Indians. Write a one-page report about the buffalo and include ways the animals were used. Draw a picture to use with your report.

4. Draw an outline map of your state/province. On the map show where various Indian tribes lived. Display this map in your classroom.

5. Pretend that you are an Indian child. Write a few paragraphs explaining your role as a member of the tribe.

6. Make a model of an Indian dwelling. Write a paragraph explaining what tribes used it and how/why this shelter was suited to a particular area.

7. Read an Indian legend. Present an oral report about it to your class.

8. Research an Indian chief. Dress as the chief and present your "autobiography" to your class.

9. Sign language is a very old means of communication. Use an encyclopedia. Learn ten different words or phrases and teach them to your class.

10. Learn an Indian song. Sing it, play it on an instrument, or use accompaniment as you perform it for your class. Share background about it with fellow students.

11. Make a diorama (shoe box scene) representing your favorite Indian tribe.

12. Collect pictures of various ways Indians traveled. Display them on a large poster in your classroom.

13. Dress a doll as an Indian. As you show it to your class, describe the costume and tell what tribe might dress in this type of clothes. (Instead of a doll, you may wish to dress yourself.)

14. Find an Indian recipe and try it. Share the "goodies" with your classmates. Copy the recipe on the board for interested students to have.

15. Make an Indian mask, shield, bow/arrow, totem pole, or other item to display in your classroom.

16. Find an Indian game. Learn it. Teach it to others in your class.

17. Preview a filmstrip or tape about Indians. Show it to your class. Create a work sheet about it. Give students the work sheet to complete. Collect handouts to grade.

18. Teach an Indian craft to your class or invite a guest speaker to share his talents with you.

19. Get a large North American map. Use a key. Label and then color each region to show where these Indians lived: Woodland, Southeastern, Plains, Pueblo, Northwest, and Canadian.

20. Create a poster-size picture dictionary of Indian words to display in the classroom. Design a pictograph using your dictionary and ask your teacher to run off several copies. Have students translate your story. Check completed work.

21. Indians were talented craftsmen. They could do painting, basketry, pottery, embroidery, metalwork, sculpture, carve, etc. Collect several of these types of items to make a "MUSEUM" for your classroom.

22. Choose a few friends. Write a script for a play about Indians. Let your teacher preview the script. Present your play to the class.

23. Make a large teepee for your classroom. Decorate it.

24. Invite an Indian to your class to share information about himself and his family.

# Tasks for the Tribe

**TO THE TEACHER:**

Here are six suggested groupings for an in-depth study of Indians by regions: (1) Eastern Woodlands (2) Southeastern Farmers (3) Plains (4) Southwest (5) Northwest (6) Canadian. Write these six groupings on the board. Choose six good student leaders to direct research groups and assign one student leader to each region. Divide the remainder of the class among the groups. Distribute copies of the GROUPINGS and the CONTRACT found on the following page. After students fill them out, collect immediately.

**TO THE GROUP LEADER:**

Try to guide your group without dictating! Be helpful! Be fair! Consult your teacher if you have a problem you cannot solve! Read all of the activities below to your group before letting students choose the particular area of study they wish to research. If your group has five members, use five topics and save topic six for one or two fast workers. With six group members, use all six topics. Try to encourage group members to keep all work neat and organized. Practice presenting all of your material within your group before sharing it with the class.

**TO THE STUDENT:**

Be an active and involved group member. Listen to your leader! Work hard each day so that your work will be done on time. Keep it neat. Be thorough in your research so that you understand your project and can explain it to your class. If you need help, ASK! Complete the project you are assigned before helping someone else. Choose one topic below and make sure your leader knows which topic it is. Don't change with a friend!

A.  LOCATION

   Draw a large map of the area where your tribe lives. Label rivers, lakes, mountains, etc. Then write a paragraph telling what the land and climate are like.

B.  SHELTER

   On poster paper draw the type of house or dwelling your tribe uses. Label it. Or make a model of that shelter. In a paragraph or two explain how the home is built and why it is suited to that region.

C.  DRESS

   Dress yourself, a doll, or draw on poster paper the clothing worn by tribe members. You may need to draw an adult male, an adult female, and a child. You may also need to include everyday clothing as well as ceremonial.

D.  TRANSPORTATION

   Draw on large paper or bring to class models showing various ways people in the tribe travel. Explain in a paragraph why this method is used in your region.

E.  FOOD

   Cut out pictures or attach small samples of food your tribe eats. Tell in a paragrah why these foods are grown/found in your region. You may want to share a recipe or a prepared "goodie" with your class.

F.  OTHER

   Include in your report or project other information about your tribe not mentioned in the above categories, such as (1) Recreation, (2) Crafts, (3) Chiefs, (4) Special Ceremonies, (5) Communications.

GROUP LEADER: _____

Members:  1. _____  2. _____  3. _____

          4. _____  5. _____  6. _____

Region of Study: _____

# *CONTRACT*

I, _____, agree to participate

in _____ Indian study group. I
will do my share to help my group research the Indians and to
present my findings to the class with my group.

I understand that all of my work is due by _____.

_____(witness) _____(date)

# WELCOME TO THE TRIBE

THIS CERTIFICATE OF HONOR IS

PRESENTED TO _____

ON THIS_____ DAY OF_____

FOR COMPLETING ALL WORK.

_____
(chief)

# "Drum" Up Some Music

**WHAT YOU NEED:**
   coffee can (1, 2 or 3 lb.)
   inner tube
   twine, heavy string, or leather shoelaces
   paper punch
   paint or construction paper
   scissors

**WHAT YOU DO:**

1.  Ask an adult to cut the top and the bottom from a coffee can.

2.  Paint an Indian design on the can OR put glue on the can and smooth construction paper around the whole can.

3.  Cut two circles from inner tube. Make each one two inches larger in diameter than the top of the can.

4.  Punch holes around the outer edge of the inner tubes approximately one inch apart using a paper punch. Don't get too close to the edge!

5.  Place one inner tube under the can and the other one on top of the can. Loosely weave the string from a hole in the bottom of the can to the top and repeat until all the holes have been laced.

6.  Gently ease up the slack in the string by feeding the string through the holes with your hands, moving in **one** direction around the can.

7.  When the drumheads are as taut as you like, secure the loose ends of the string carefully.

**NOTE:**
A.  Various-sized drums make different sounds.
B.  Sounds will vary, too, if you loosen or tighten the drumheads.
C.  You can create various patterns by tapping your drum with your fingertips, your palms, or sticks. Be creative!

# NATIVE NECKLACES

MIX ½ cup of water and a small amount of plaster of Paris in a small container. The mixture should be as thick as pudding. Using a spoon, put a small walnut-sized portion of moist plaster of Paris on a piece of waxed paper.

SHAPE it into a design suitable for beads or an Indian medallion. *Carefully put a hole near the top as shown. Let the shape harden. Sandpaper it until smooth.

PAINT with tempera or poster paint. If desired, the pendant could be given a coat of clear, colorless nail polish or clear varnish.

STRING the pendant on a chain, ribbon, yarn or leather string!

# THE STAR AND THE LILY

## Characters:

| | |
|---|---|
| NARRATOR | WARRIOR 4 |
| OLD CHIEF | WARRIOR 5 |
| CHILDREN (about 6) | WISE MAN 1 |
| ANIMALS (as many as you wish) | WISE MAN 2 |
| CRIER | WISE MAN 3 |
| WARRIOR 1 | WISE MAN 4 |
| WARRIOR 2 | BRIGHT STAR |
| WARRIOR 3 | YOUNG MAIDEN |

**Stage Directions:** On the left side of the stage as you face it or off to one corner near the stage, seat OLD CHIEF near a teepee.

On the right side of the stage, stand BRIGHT STAR on something tall so that he will appear in the sky. Put a large poster paper star on the front and the back of a student to play the character of BRIGHT STAR.

NARRATOR:    Welcome to our play entitled "The Star and the Lily."

OLD CHIEF:    (Sitting near his teepee enjoying the sun.)

CHILDREN:    (Playing nearby and skip to the OLD CHIEF.) Tell us a story! Tell us a story! (They gather around him as he begins.)

ANIMALS:    (Enter slowly, a few at a time and scamper about the stage while the OLD CHIEF speaks.)

OLD CHIEF:    Long ago our land was filled with the scurry of animals across the plains and in the forest, fearing nothing. Our people were happy people, all the Indian nations were as one, and there were no wars. It was a beautiful time when only the Indians inhabited the wilderness. In the quiet of the night they would gather in the fields and watch the stars. (Lights dim; spotlight BRIGHT STAR.)

WARRIORS, WISE MEN, CRIER: (Enter and sit in clusters on stage looking toward the sky at BRIGHT STAR. They pretend to whisper among themselves.)

WARRIOR 1:    That star is so bright it surely cannot be too far away!

WARRIOR 2:    See how close to the tree it seems!

WARRIORS:    (Walk slowly toward BRIGHT STAR.)

WARRIOR 3:    It looks like a bird!

WARRIORS:    (Return to the circle of seated friends.)

WARRIORS, WISE MEN: (Talk softly among themselves.)

WISE MEN:        We must go see for ourselves!

WISE MAN 1:      And so it does appear like a bird!

WISE MEN:        (Stand near star and whisper among themselves.)

WISE MAN 2:      I think it is a sign of a terrible war coming! The sign our forefathers spoke of.

WISE MAN 3:      I think it must be a good omen, a sign of something good!

WISE MEN:        (Return to the cluster of friends, talk about the star, and then exit from the stage—WARRIOR 4 remains on stage, stares a few moments at the star, and then falls asleep.)

YOUNG MAIDEN:    (Standing near WARRIOR 4 and speaking softly.) Young Brave, I have left my sisters in the sky so that I might come live with you always. Please ask your WARRIORS and WISE MEN what form I should take so I may live here and be loved!

WARRIOR 4:       (Awakens and looks at BRIGHT STAR.)

CRIER:           (Knows nothing of the dream but comes to tell WARRIOR 4 of a council meeting.) I must find the other WARRIORS and WISE MEN and tell them of our meeting!

WARRIORS and WISE MEN: (Enter and gather in a circle seated on center stage.)

WARRIOR 4:       (Stands and tells others of this dream.) Last night as I slept I dreamed a beautiful maiden spoke to me. "Young brave," she said, "I have left my sisters so that I might come live with you always. Please ask your WARRIORS and WISE MEN what form I should take so that I may live here and be loved!"

WARRIOR 5:       I think that BRIGHT STAR has fallen in love with mankind.

WISE MAN 4:      I agree! And it sounds as though she wants to live on earth!

WARRIORS AND WISE MEN: (Short soft discussion and they exit from stage.)

WARRIORS:        (Enter and stand near star and hold up a peace pipe as a welcome to BRIGHT STAR to EARTH. WARRIORS walk home and BRIGHT STAR follows. All WARRIORS exit except WARRIOR 4 who falls asleep again on stage.)

YOUNG MAIDEN:    (Appears to WARRIOR 4.) Young brave, where can I live? What form shall I take?

WARRIOR 4:       (Talking to YOUNG MAIDEN.) You could live in the flowers, or in a tree, or on top of the hill by the meadow! **You** choose the place!

YOUNG MAIDEN:    (Searches around on stage to find a home.) I know where I'll live! I wish to see the gliding canoes of the people I love the most. (And she sits in the water and looks at her reflection.)

WISE MEN:        (Pretend to paddle cardboard canoe. Secretly they place several white tissue flowers in the water.)

NARRATOR:        When you see this lily on the water (holds up white tissue flower), gently pick it up and lift it toward the skies, so that it will be as happy on this earth as its sisters, the morning and evening stars, who remain happy in the heavens.

---

* Based on an Ojibwa legend from a story by the same title, published in *Indian Legends of the Sky, Earth, and Man* by William Wagner (Indianapolis, Ind.: Youth Publication/Saturday Evening Post Co., 1978).

# PLAY TIME

Read the play carefully. Then answer the questions below.

1. What makes a story a play? _____

   _____

2. What is meant by characters? _____

3. Where are the directions or actions for the characters written? _____

   _____

4. Another word for the manuscript of the play is called the script. Which words in the

   script are meant to be spoken aloud? _____

5. Why should you read a play first before you choose a character you would like to por-

   tray? _____

   _____

6. How can you remember YOUR cue, or signal, to speak? _____

   _____

7. What is meant by the PROPS in a play? _____

   _____

8. There are two parts in this play in which the number of characters can be easily chang-

   ed. Which two parts are they? _____

9. Which WARRIOR has a dream? _____

10. What is meant by CRIER? _____

    _____

11. What is the purpose of OLD CHIEF in this play? _____

    _____

12. The WISE MEN and WARRIORS thought that BRIGHT STAR looked like a _____.

13. Name at least three props that could be used in this play. _____

    _____

14. At the close of the play, BRIGHT STAR took the form of _____,

    and she chose to live in_____.

# SIOUX SHUFFLE

Although this dance is designed for approximately 20-30 students, adapt it to the class size you have by varying the number of drummers. You might also want to use rhythm sticks, tambourines, and shakers for accompaniment, therefore using additional pupils.

Seat drummers/musicians (about 5) in the center of the stage or performing area. Stand the remainder of the class in a large circle around them. Choose one leader for the drummers and one for the dancers. Then follow the directions below or create/supplement with ideas of your own appropriate to your grade level. Dance movements will change when the drum pattern changes. This will be determined by the DRUM LEADER! Select a responsible child.

DRUMMERS     (pattern 1): Tap once with right hand and wait three more beats; repeat as often as desired.

DANCERS     (pattern 1): Step hop right, step hop left, moving clockwise around circle until drum pattern changes. Follow your DANCE LEADER!

DRUMMERS     (pattern 2): Tap once with right hand, wait one beat; repeat as often as desired.

DANCERS     (pattern 2): Step hop right, step hop left, moving counterclockwise around circle until drum pattern changes.

DRUMMERS     (pattern 3): Tap all four beats on the drum. Right hand taps loudly followed by three softer beats of the left hand; repeat as often as desired.

DANCERS     (pattern 3): Circle in place to the right two times; then circle in place to the left two times; continue this pattern until the drum pattern changes.

DRUMMERS     (pattern 4): Tap **loudly** with both hands, continuously.

DANCERS     (pattern 4): Entire circle of dancers faces the center and walks forward four steps with waving arms upward, then walks backwards four steps with arms extended forward toward center and body bent forward at waist; repeat until drum pattern changes.

DRUMMERS     (pattern 5): Tap **softly** with both hands continuously, then fade out.

DANCERS     (pattern 5): With backs to the drummers, walk clockwise making a complete circle around musicians; repeat motion walking counterclockwise; turn to face drummers; raise hands high overhead and wiggle arms for eight beats; bend over and wiggle arms toward center for eight beats; stoop down and put arms at side with heads bowed. Remain in this position until drums fade to signal program end.

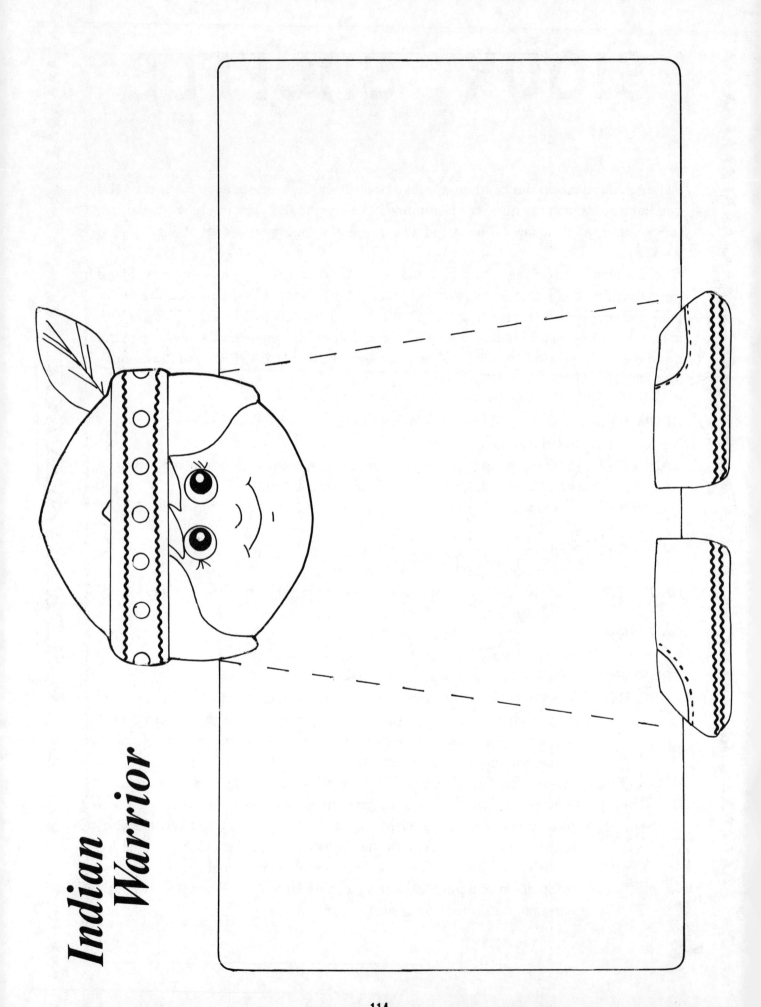

Indian
Warrior

114

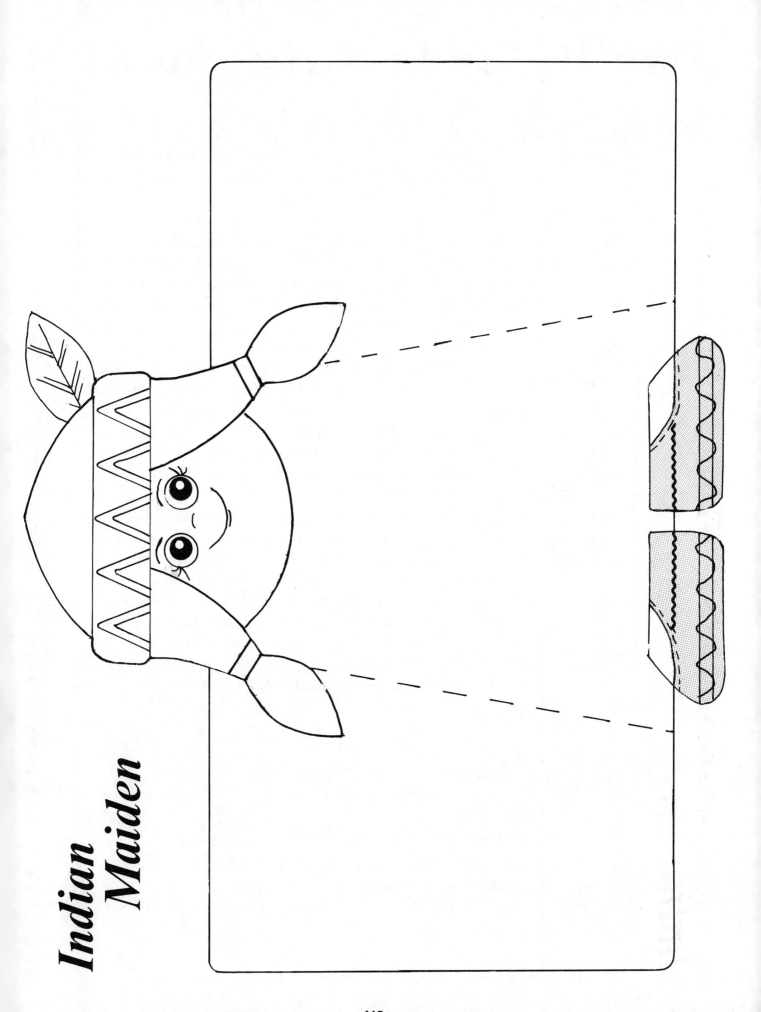

Indian Maiden

115

# We'll Entertain You !

**PREPARATION:**

Costumes: Moccasins, T-shirts, dark pants, burlap sack dresses (belted), jewelry, headbands, feathers, makeup (paint), bows/arrows, shields, dolls dressed for papooses

Music: Drums, shakers (gourds), wooden rhythm sticks

Projects: Arrange completed student projects around performing area so that students or group leaders can explain charts, maps, posters, reports, or other areas of research. This will not only add atmosphere, but will supplement the Indian program with background information.

Invitations: Use the Indian Maiden pattern (page 115). Have students write an invitation on the inside of the paper asking other teachers to bring their classes to your program. Review how to write invitations with your class, or write a sample one on the board for students to copy.

Programs: Use the Indian Warrior pattern provided (page 114). Write the agenda for the program on the board for children to copy in their best writing.

Helpers: Assign students to: (1) emcee the entire program; (2) place necklaces (medallions) on all of the students in the class who participated in the Indian unit of study (could call students by any Indian names they choose); (3) present projects to the group (could use several students or group leaders only); (4) make props for the play; (5) one student leads the dancers and another student leads the drummers; (6) distribute invitations to various teachers; (7) pass out copies of the program (perhaps to only the adults attending the presentation).

**PROGRAM:**
1. Welcome
2. Presentation of Projects
3. Necklace Ceremony
4. Play: "The Star and the Lily"
5. Sioux Shuffle
6. Thank You (please feel free to browse through the projects, etc.)

**NOTE:** Please understand that these are only suggestions. Feel free to add or delete ideas suitable for your classroom.

# MY DOOR KNOCKER

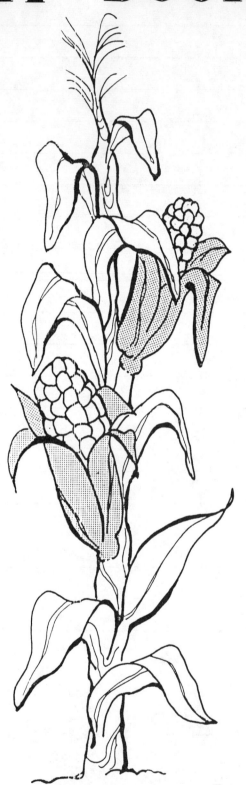

Your classroom door will look quite attractive with this fall decoration. Title it "Ear Ye! Ear Ye!"

Make a large cornstalk from shelf or butcher paper. Color it before it is laminated. Attach it to the outside of your classroom door.

Give each student a copy of the ear of corn pattern found on the next page. Have each child color his corn, cut it out, write a "corny joke" on the husk, and then sign his name before he gives it to his teacher to be displayed on the cornstalk.

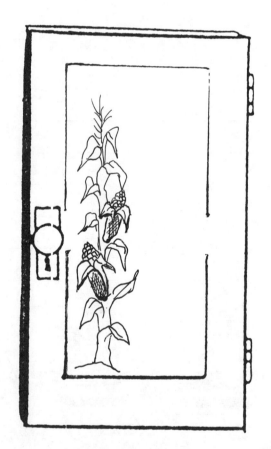

118

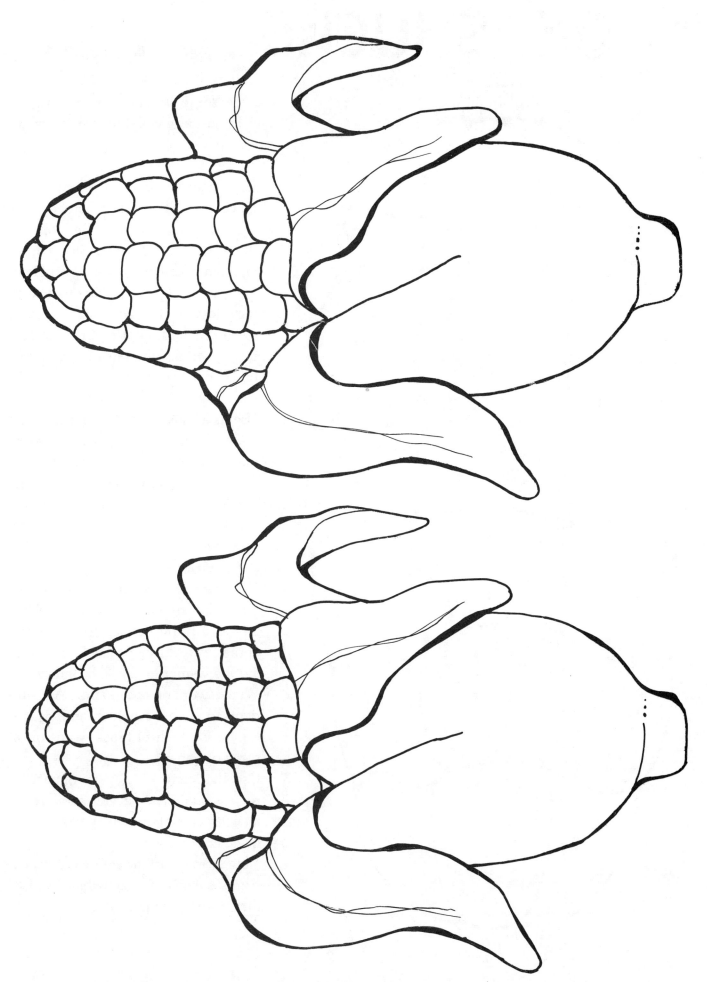

# OH SHUCKS.....

Here are some versatile games and activities for just a few players or your entire class!

**Math:**

1. Give each student an ear of corn. Have him write a number between 1-30 on each kernel. Use popcorn (unpopped) for markers. Give a mental math operation (5 x 2 + 3). Have the student place a marker on the correct answer. Players can win by a covered board, vertical, or horizontal row covered with markers. For variety, change the set of numbers you will use, change the operation, etc.

2. Use as a station for individuals. Laminate several ears of corn. On each one write various numbers, making each ear different. (Because they're laminated, you can use them for other activities.) Have children add rows of numbers, etc.

**Language Arts:**

1. Give each child an ear of corn. Have him write any eighteen of his spelling words for the week, one in each kernel. Play the game like Bingo, asking the winner to say "Oh Shucks."

2. Write a word on each kernel. Ask students to write a synonym and/or antonym for each of those words on a piece of paper.

3. Use the corn for a parts-of-speech review. Laminate several ears. Then let children write nouns, verbs, adjectives, etc., on each kernel.

4. You decide or let the students create a game suitable to something which they are studying.

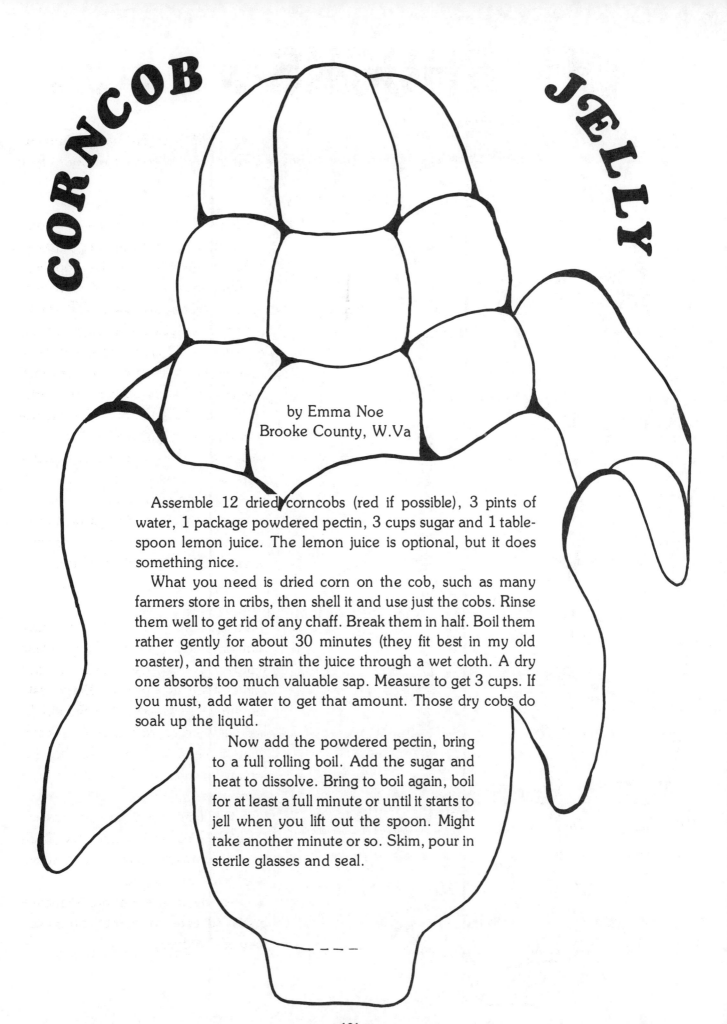

# CORNCOB JELLY

by Emma Noe
Brooke County, W.Va

Assemble 12 dried corncobs (red if possible), 3 pints of water, 1 package powdered pectin, 3 cups sugar and 1 tablespoon lemon juice. The lemon juice is optional, but it does something nice.

What you need is dried corn on the cob, such as many farmers store in cribs, then shell it and use just the cobs. Rinse them well to get rid of any chaff. Break them in half. Boil them rather gently for about 30 minutes (they fit best in my old roaster), and then strain the juice through a wet cloth. A dry one absorbs too much valuable sap. Measure to get 3 cups. If you must, add water to get that amount. Those dry cobs do soak up the liquid.

Now add the powdered pectin, bring to a full rolling boil. Add the sugar and heat to dissolve. Bring to boil again, boil for at least a full minute or until it starts to jell when you lift out the spoon. Might take another minute or so. Skim, pour in sterile glasses and seal.

# Answer Key

## Page 8
1. 176
2. 282
3. 289
4. 188
5. 136
6. 539
7. 324
8. 359

## Page 13
1. Spelling book
2. Blue book
3. Cookbook
4. Red book
5. Webster's Dictionary
6. Student's name
7. _____ Mystery
8. 1-10 Yellow
9. Teacher's name

## Page 23
Walt—$2.00
Ann—$1.25
Judy—$1.75

## Page 49
$82.93 before sales tax. Determine your own tax for your class.

## Page 50
1. $12.34
2. $13.75
3. $12.87
4. $14.12
5. $15.13
6. $13.64
7. $12.30
8. $13.72
9. $13.41

Tree #5 makes more cents.

## Page 54

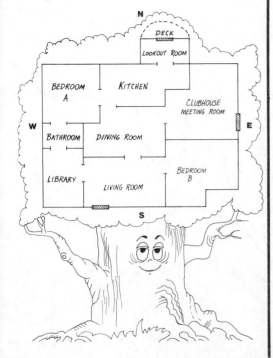

## Page 56

Crossword:
ORCHARD NURSERY PAPER
PHOTOSYNTHESIS CACAO
BRANCH CROWN
OAK CROWN EVERGREEN
SEED OAK MAPLE FLOWER
CHLOROPHYLL
SEQUOIA TULIP BUD FRUIT
PALM THORNS
SAGUARO HICKORY

## Page 60
1. Aspen
2. Elm
3. Carob
4. Mango
5. Oak
6. Ash
7. Maple
8. Palm
9. Willow
10. Poplar
11. Gum
12. Beech
13. Pear
14. Pine
15. Camphor
16. Evergreen
17. Rubber
18. Teak

## Page 62
1. there
2. where
3. little
4. middle
5. it
6. sit
7. bit
8. way
9. day
10. play
11. tree
12. especially
13. be
14. she
15. me
16. you
17. too
18. view
19. into
20. do
21. to
22. my
23. high
24. nearby
25. try
26. I
27. when
28. then
29. been
30. call
31. all
32. yard
33. hard
34. take
35. make

## Page 77
1. Noun
2. Verb
3. Verb
4. Noun
5. Verb
6. Verb
7. Noun
8. Noun

## Page 78
1. I watched TV.
2. We put up a new fence last year.
3. The lifeguard blew her whistle.
4. My little brother can't read very well.
5. Uncle Joe lives nearby.
6. I can play soccer, too.

## Page 89
1. 13
2. 80
3. 52
4. 161
5. $12.94
   $2.06
6. 38

## Page 92
1. 5,016
2. 39,220
3. 17,005
4. 12,184
5. 37,590
6. 7,317
7. 25,705
8. 9,758
9. 25,110
10. 7948
11. 19,325

## Page 112
1. the format which gives speaking/acting parts to various characters
2. people or objects in the play
3. in parentheses beside characters' names
4. words not in parentheses
5. to get to know him and choose a part you can play best
6. Listen for words of the character before you.
7. objects needed for scenery or for characters to use
8. children and animals
9. 4
10. one who goes around on foot announcing messages
11. storyteller who unfolds the legend presented
12. bird
13. peace pipe, canoe, tissue flowers (water lilies), teepee
14. water lily; the water (where gliding canoes see reflection)